TOP
DIVE SITES OF
AUSTRALIA

BECCA SAUNDERS

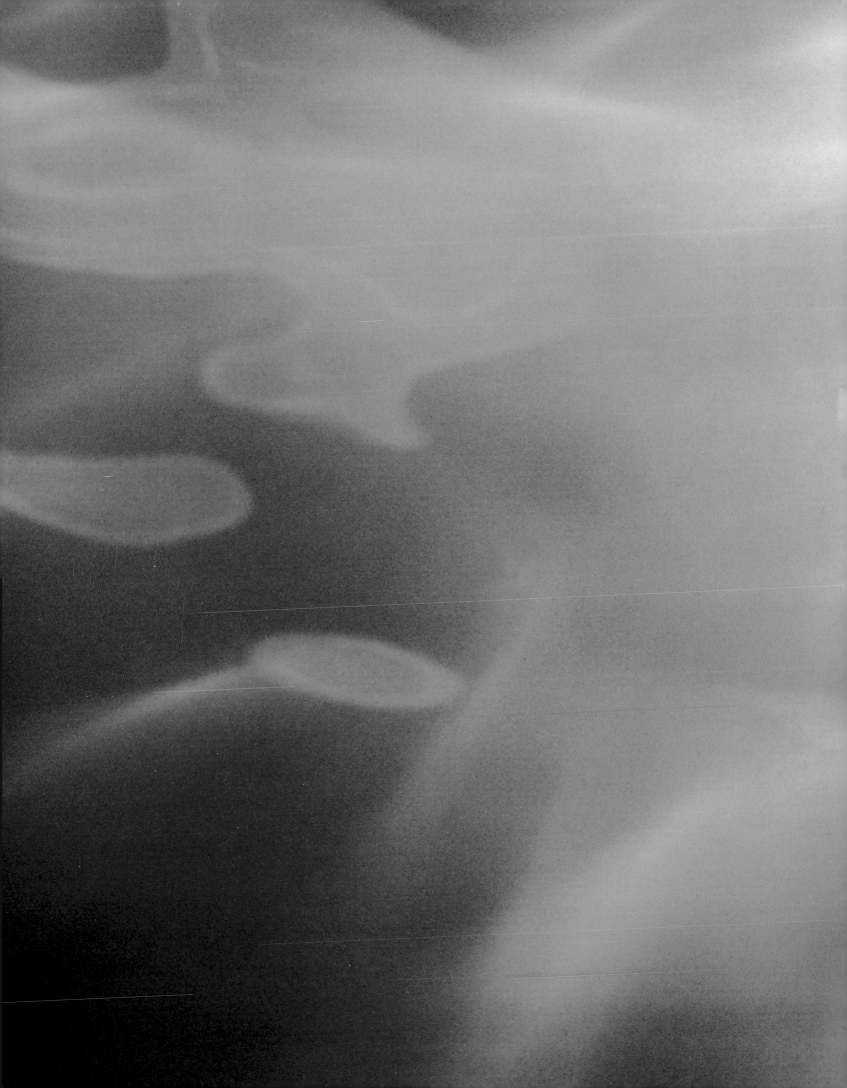

TOP
DIVE SITES OF
AUSTRALIA

BECCA SAUNDERS

First published in Australia in 2001 by

New Holland Publishers (Australia) Pty Ltd

Sydney • Auckland • London • Cape Town

14 Aquatic Drive Frenchs Forest NSW 2086 Australia

218 Lake Road Northcote Auckland New Zealand

86 Edgware Road London W2 2EA United Kingdom

80 McKenzie Street Cape Town 8001 South Africa

National Library of Australia Cataloguing-in-Publication Data:

Saunders, Rebecca East.

Top dive sites of Australia

Includes index.

ISBN 1 86436 592 7

1. Skin diving—Australia—Guidebooks.

2. Deep diving—Australia—Guidebooks.

3. Scuba diving—Australia—Guidebooks. I. Title.

797.23

Publishing Manager: Anouska Good

Senior Editor: Monica Ban

Copy Editor: Sam Chapman

Designer: Peta Nugent

Layout: Nanette Backhouse and Jenny Mansfield

Map illustrator: Nicole Struik

Production: Janelle Smith

Reproduction: Pica

Printer: Imago, Singapore

This book was typeset in Arrus BT 10 pt

Cover: Large trout and colourful corals at Rowley Shoals.

Back cover: Nudibranch on a sea fan at Rowley Shoals.

Page 5: Brilliant jewel anemones are common throughout south-east Australia.

Page 6: Divers enjoy a safety stop in the clear warm waters of Rowley Shoals.

Page 9: Tiny 'sea fleas' are temperate water animals and were once featured on a postage stamp!

TO MARK

CONTENTS

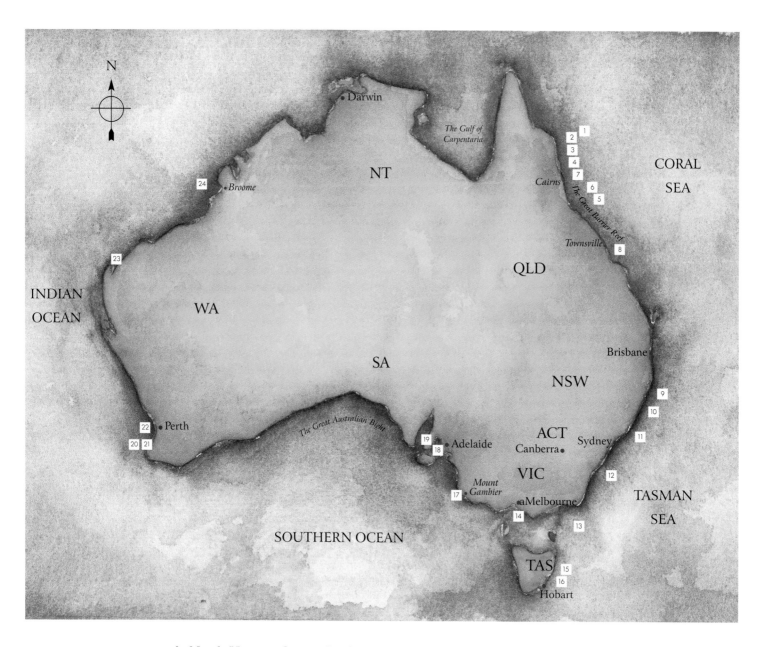

1. North Horn at Osprey Reef
2. The Cod Hole
3. Pixie's Pinnacle
4. Minke Whales
5. Scuba Zoo
6. Flinders Reef
7. Mass Spawning
8. The Wreck of the SS *Yongala*
9. The Solitary Islands
10. South West Rocks
11. Seal Rocks
12. Jervis Bay

13. Wilsons Promontory
14. Port Phillip Heads and Submarines
15. Bicheno
16. Eaglehawk
17. Cave Diving in Mount Gambier
18. Rapid Bay Jetty
19. White Sharks
20. The Wreck of the HMAS *Swan*
21. Busselton Jetty
22. Rottnest Island
23. Whale Sharks
24. Rowley Shoals

INTRODUCTION

Australia is blessed with the most spectacular diving in the world. From the far north of Queensland right around the continent to the far north of Western Australia, we have it all...tropical splendour, mysterious temperate water environments, shipwrecks, kelp forests, and cave diving. We have sharks the size of whales, whales the size of large dolphins, giant cuttlefish, fish that walk, and the only two species of seadragons in the world. Divers come from all over the globe to sample our underwater delights and they invariably leave overwhelmed with the magnitude and scope of the Australian dive scene.

Top Dive Sites of Australia presents a cross-section of Australia's most popular diving. In some cases a whole area is presented, in other cases a single site merits a chapter all to itself. In-depth descriptions, colour photographs, plus extensive travel tips combine to enchant experienced divers while whetting the appetites of novice divers as well as those who have yet to take 'the plunge'.

Selecting the sites for this book was difficult and I apologise in advance to all the dive sites which did not get included. Ask 100 divers what the best sites are in Australia and you'll get 100 different answers. I couldn't begin to cover all the great diving available in this country, but this book is a good representative cross-section.

If I had my way, *Top Dive Sites of Australia* would be twice as long and contain many more pictures, but budgets are budgets and I've tried to cram as much information as I can into the allotted pages. But there's always plenty more to say and readers might want to visit my web site occasionally at www.australia-downunder-productions.com, for updates, extended travel tips and new operator contact details.

To all who travel with me through this book, may your seas be calm, your water clear and your animals cooperative. Safe diving!

Becca Saunders

Becca Saunders

NORTH HORN
AT OSPREY REEF

ABOVE: A barracuda
often rests under boats
moored at North Horn.

OPPOSITE: North Horn is
famous for its healthy
shark population.

Osprey Reef lies 310 kilometres north-east of Port Douglas, Queensland, and is the most northerly of the Coral Sea reefs. It is 21 kilometres long and 4 kilometres wide and features a large lagoon offering safe anchorage for visiting liveaboard charter boats. Situated on the north-east tip of Osprey Reef is a dive site called North Horn, world famous for its exceptionally clear water, large fans, huge soft coral trees, and lots and lots of sharks.

Unlike most dive sites on Osprey Reef which are vertical walls, North Horn features a shelf which gently slopes down to about 40 metres before turning into a vertical wall plunging down forever. Jumping in for the first time, divers are usually confronted with a landscape of sharks. Dozens of whalers patrol the walls and the deeper water under the boat, while North Horn's permanent colony of whitetip reef sharks swarm over the sloping reef.

The shelf itself is encrusted in corals, sea whips, fans, soft corals and lots of fish. Several fat, cheeky potato cod live on North Horn and they have no problems with literally bumping divers to let them know that they're there and they'd like a free feed. Often, a cod will choose a buddy pair and follow them throughout the dive, peering over their shoulders to see what they're looking at and usually sticking their big, boofy heads in front of camera lenses at exactly the wrong moment.

The Coral Sea is famous for its colourful soft coral trees and North Horn is no exception. On the west side of the point, there is a grove of soft coral starting in about 18 metres and continuing on to 40+ metres. Huge and vibrant, in shades of red, pink, orange, purple and yellow, the deeper you go, the larger and more impressive the specimen. Nestled in amongst the branches, you can sometimes find tiny commensal crabs, cowries and nudibranchs which perfectly mimic the soft coral polyps.

Before leaving the extreme depths, take a few minutes to swim away from the wall and hang in the blue water. If you breathe quietly and remain motionless, you might see schooling hammerheads (in winter and early spring), huge dogtooth tuna, manta rays, eagle rays, schooling barracuda and maybe even an oceanic whitetip shark.

Working your way back up the reef, check out the shallower areas. Large fissures cut deeply into the reef and often provide sanctuary for resting pelagics such as blue-fin

trevally. Divers with keen eyes frequently find perfectly camouflaged leaf fish in tiny holes or under ledges, and the whole area is speckled with a variety of colourful anemones and anemonefish. Safety stops can easily be carried out while poking around on the reef, but save a little air for a quick turn under the boat. Large schools of fish often shelter there and sometimes you'll find a giant barracuda lurking in the shadow.

And then, of course, there are the shark feeds, which are conducted on a small pinnacle called the Pulpit located in 14 metres of water. Guests jump in first and scatter themselves along the wall on the reef side of the pinnacle, leaving the ocean side clear for approaching sharks. Once everyone is in place, the crew jumps in with milk crates stuffed full of tuna heads and frames.

Within seconds of hitting the water, the whitetip contingency are all over the bait, escorting it all the way to the Pulpit where it is attached to a permanent mooring chain. Right in the middle of the ruckus are the potato cod which have no fear of sharks, even during a feeding frenzy. Circling grey reef whalers gradually build up the courage to come in, but the extremely cautious silvertips normally approach only after 10 or 15 minutes of watching from a safe distance. On occasion, 40-kilogram tuna shoot through, grabbing a bite as they pass by, and in winter, scallops and great hammerheads make the occasional appearance.

Osprey Reef is also the site of several ongoing research projects hosted by the *Undersea Explorer*, a liveaboard charter boat well-known for its active participation in various marine research projects. One program is a dynamic study

of the resident whitetip reef sharks. Passive research such as observation, counting and photo-graphing takes place on every trip to Osprey Reef. This information is used to investigate growth rates, the location and times of breeding, behavioural patterns, and movements.

Several times a year, the *Undersea Explorer* hosts shark tagging expeditions. Supervised by Australia's top shark scientists, whitetip reef sharks are attracted by a contained bait bin placed underwater. North Horn is so sharky, that actual feeding isn't required to bring sharks in close. The mere presence of bait in the water, even if it is inaccessible, is enough to draw several dozen sharks to the Pulpit area.

Once a good group of sharks has congregated, experienced shark handlers select an ani-mal, throw a loop around its tail and gently raise the shark to the dive platform on the back of the boat. Here, the animal is checked for existing subdermal tags. If it is a new specimen, a tag is inserted in a method similar to microchipping dogs and cats. Measurements are taken, statistics are recorded and a small sample of tissue is taken and preserved for DNA finger-printing. Then the shark is released.

ABOVE: North Horn has a permanent colony of whitetip reef sharks.

OPPOSITE LEFT: Perfectly camouflaged cowries live on giant soft coral trees.

OPPOSITE RIGHT: Scientists measuring and microchipping a shark.

Occasionally, a whitetip will be fitted with an ultrasonic transmitter. Several have already been implanted and these animals are being tracked by fixed underwater computer dataloggers which record their movements throughout the year. This information, when combined with the weekly and sometimes twice-weekly visual observations made by onboard science officers, provides details about the animals' home range, feeding and breeding times, and movements.

For obvious reasons, guests cannot participate in the hands-on activities of capturing and tagging, but they are welcome to watch, either in the water or from the boat, and in-depth slide shows are presented to guests each afternoon explaining what's happening, why they're doing it and what observations have been made to date.

Another research project hosted by the *Undersea Explorer* on Osprey Reef is a nautilus survey. Once or twice a week, two large wire traps are set in 200 metres of water and left overnight. The next morning, the traps are retrieved, and in most cases, anywhere from six to twelve nautiluses are collected.

Being deep water animals, nautiluses need cold water to survive and the collected animals are kept in refrigerated tanks for the day before being released that evening. Each nautilus is tagged by scratching an area of the shell, labelling with a marker, and covering the label with clear nail lacquer. Photographs and measurements are taken, then the animals are released in the late afternoon, escorted by guests as they move back to their more familiar depths.

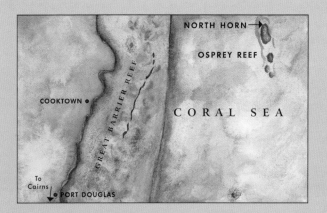

Of the nautiluses caught since early 1997, there has been almost a 6 per cent recapture rate, which compares favourably with other nautilus mark and recapture programs. These recaptures have occurred between one and 27 months after the initial capture, giving confidence in both the tagging method and the viability of released animals.

Guests are invited to assist in the trapping, tagging and data collecting activities, and slide shows detailing the research program are presented. Several times a year, Australia's top cephalopod scientists travel with guests on the *Undersea Explorer* to participate in the weekly surveys as well as conduct research and experiments on other cephalopods. Guests are encouraged to participate in these experiments.

Osprey Reef is remote, and it's a long trip across open sea to get there. The crossing can be rough, and divers with weak stomachs should stock up on seasick tablets before leaving shore. Certainly, there's a price to pay for diving perfection, but the clear water, beautiful corals and guaranteed sharks at North Horn, along with the opportunity to participate in various research projects, make the effort well worthwhile.

ABOVE: Research at North Horn gives divers an opportunity to see a live nautilus.

OPPOSITE: Magnificent soft coral trees are a main feature of Osprey Reef. a

TRAVEL TIPS

GETTING THERE: Located over 300 kilometres north of Port Douglas, Osprey Reef can only be dived via liveaboard charters. Choose operators based in Port Douglas or Cairns.

BEST TIME TO GO: The rainy season is in summer (January–March). The windy season is in winter (April–July). Diving is great all year round but the calmest, driest weather is between August and December.

CLIMATE: 21–31°C early summer through autumn (October–April), 18–26°C in winter through early spring (May–September). January and February are the warmest months. July and August are the coldest months. These temperatures are for Cairns; it will always be cooler at sea.

WATER TEMPERATURES: 27–29°C during October–March and most divers wear 3mm wetsuits. 24–26°C during April–September and most divers wear 5mm wetsuits.

VISIBILITY: Averages 30+ metres and can frequently exceed 60 metres.

SNORKELLING: Excellent. Even the shark interactions can be watched from the surface.

OPERATORS

UNDERSEA EXPLORER (out of Port Douglas)
Tel: (07) 4099 5911, Fax: (07) 4099 5914
Email: undersea@ozemail.com.au
Internet: www.underseaexplorer.com

TAKA DIVE AUSTRALIA (out of Cairns)
Tel: (07) 4051 8722, Fax: (07) 4031 2739
Email: takadive@taka.com.au
Internet: www.taka.com.au

THE COD HOLE

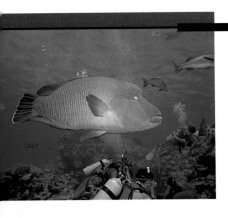

ABOVE: Shy Maori wrasse
circle divers but keep
their distance.

OPPOSITE: Potato cod
frequently come almost
to the surface.

The Ribbon Reefs are a string of ten sinuous coral ramparts stretching along the outer edge of the northern Great Barrier Reef in Queensland. Referred to as Ribbon Reef Numbers 1 through 10 (from south to north), the Ribbons are rarely wider than 500 metres and can be up to 25 kilometres long. The eastern faces of the reefs feature plunging walls, which go down hundreds of metres. The western sides feature shallow, sloping reefs with gutters, bommies and coral gardens. Separating each ribbon are narrow deep passages, home to strong currents and amazing underwater pinnacles thick with colourful marine life. At the northern tip of Ribbon #10, is the world famous Cod Hole.

The Cod Hole began as a sheltered area where fishermen cleaned their catches, throwing the scraps and offal overboard. It didn't take the local cod, Maori wrasse and giant moray eels long to work out what a good deal that was and over the years they have congregated in larger and larger numbers.

In the early 1970s, pioneering divers heard rumours of the Cod Hole and set out to investigate. What they found was nothing short of amazing. Dozens of huge potato cod, some weighing over 150 kilograms, had made the area their home and what was even more amazing was that they had no fear of divers. Recognising the importance of the site, the original divers lobbied hard and succeeded in having the area declared a protected site.

By the middle 1980s, the Cod Hole had become a well-known dive site and was considered a 'must do' dive for all liveaboard dive boats travelling through the area. Even two decades on, the Cod Hole is still one of the most popular dive sites on the Great Barrier Reef.

The Cod Hole is a collection of bommies and gutters. The coral nearly breaks the surface at its shallowest point, and the deepest areas, further out on the sand, average around 20 metres. Being adjacent to a channel, currents can be quite strong, but divers can shelter in the sandy patches and holes which contribute to the site's name.

With thousands of divers visiting the area every year and most of them scrambling around on the reef trying to interact with the cod, the surrounding coral is fairly dead and the terrain looks like a bomb site. But divers don't go there to see coral, they go there to see huge, approachable fish.

TOP LEFT: Large moray eels need to be treated with caution.

TOP CENTRE: Nudibranchs can be found in protected areas on the reef.

TOP RIGHT: Cod move from diver to diver looking for food.

Most formal feeding is done in one of the shallow, sandy holes which is protected from the current. The cod appear as soon as the divers jump in and swim inquiringly from diver to diver as the group descends to the feeding area. Off in the distance, shyer Maori wrasse circle. Even after years of feeding, these big fish are still shy and rarely, if ever, interact with divers the way the cod do.

On arriving at the feeding station, guests settle quietly in a large circle trying hard to avoid stirring up the bottom which is a fine, silty sand. At this point, the potato cod are still swimming from diver to diver, trying to figure out who has the food. Smaller greasy cod quietly take up positions around the perimeter of the sandy patch. Being less aggressive, they don't like being in the middle of the fray. Instead, they live in hope that a morsel will be dropped by one of the bigger fish.

Finally, the divemaster arrives with the bait and the cod start squabbling for prime position. Fat, overfed and aggressive, there's always a dominant cod which often literally bowls over divers and smaller fish alike in an attempt to land in the prime position next to the bait box. Agitated and ready to take on all interlopers, the dominant cod snaps at intruding fish, and on occasion, simply eats any small fish which venture too close!

The actual feeding happens very quickly. Using large pieces of bait, the divemaster surreptitiously removes a hunk of fish from the box and quickly throws it upward. The large cod literally inhale the food, opening their mouths in nanoseconds and sucking the bait in. While they don't have actual teeth, their sheer size makes them dangerous. Cod have been known to accidentally bite hands and even swallow dive gloves, so feeding should be left in the capable hands of well-trained guides.

The dominant cod gets most of the food, but if the guide is sneaky and quick, sometimes the smaller cod and the ever-patient greasy cod will also get a bite.

Large morays used to be a real feature of the site. Getting fed regularly, these eels grew to tremendous sizes, sometimes as big as a man's thigh. But morays have very sharp teeth and incidents regularly occurred. On one occasion, a dive guide, wearing only a speedo and a loose, jacket-style BCD, had the pleasure of a large, agitated moray swimming up between his body and his BCD and staring him in the face. When a divemaster lost her arm in the mid-1990s after being bitten several times by a large moray, most of the eels were removed from the site.

Even without food, the cod are very approachable and many charter boats choose not to put on a formal feed. In these cases, divers simply jump in and swim around. More often than not, the dominant cod will spend the entire dive swimming from diver to diver, trying to assess who has food and who doesn't. Often, a single smaller cod will stay with a buddy pair for the whole dive, even following them up the anchor line to the back of the boat.

Located in a channel which enjoys good, cleansing currents, the Cod Hole often plays host to other large animals, including trevally, barracuda, mackerel, whitetip reef sharks, manta rays and even turtles. Closer to the rocks are blue-spotted rays, anemonefish and nudibranchs.

The Cod Hole also offers excellent night diving, provided the currents aren't too strong. The sandy bottom is the perfect spot to see shellfish and starfish out for an evening stroll.

The concept of feeding wild animals is hotly debated and how well the animals survive the experience is also an issue. Over the years, the quantity of potato cod at the Cod Hole has dwindled and the health of the animals has decreased, with cankers and skin diseases becoming evident, most probably due to handling by divers. It is important that boats give full briefings prior to any dives, outlining safety procedures and proper cod-interaction etiquette.

While there are certainly fewer fish at the Cod Hole than there were years ago, even one or two giant potato cod will make for an exciting underwater experience, particularly for divers who have had few, if any, encounters with large, approachable fish. Even after two decades of heavy diving, the Cod Hole is still considered one of Australia's top underwater attractions and is well worth a visit.

TRAVEL TIPS

GETTING THERE: Located 270 kilometres north of Cairns and 190 kilometres north of Port Douglas, the Cod Hole can only be dived via liveaboard charters.

BEST TIME TO GO: All year round.

CLIMATE: 21–31°C late spring through autumn (October–April), 18–26°C in winter through early spring (May–September). January and February are the warmest months. July and August are the coldest months. These temperatures are for Cairns; it will always be cooler at sea.

WATER TEMPERATURES: 27–29°C October–March, most divers wear 3mm wetsuits. 24–26°C during April–September, most divers wear 5mm wetsuits.

VISIBILITY: 15–30 metres.

SNORKELLING: The Cod Hole offers excellent snorkelling with cod frequently coming almost to the surface.

OPERATORS

Most liveaboard dive charters cruising the Ribbon Reefs will visit the Cod Hole, including:

UNDERSEA EXPLORER (out of Port Douglas)
Tel: (07) 4099 5911, Fax: (07) 4099 5914
Email: undersea@ozemail.com.au
Internet: www.underseaexplorer.com

RUM RUNNER (out of Cairns)
Tel: (07) 4050 9988, Fax: (07) 4050 9911
Email: reservations@rumrunner.com.au
Internet: www.rumrunner.com.au

MIKE BALL DIVE EXPEDITIONS (out of Cairns)
Tel: (07) 4031 5484, Fax: (07) 4031 5470
Email: mbde@mikeball.com
Internet: www.mikeball.com

PIXIE'S PINNACLE

ABOVE: Leather coral polyps extended in the current for feeding.

OPPOSITE: Every crevice is packed with corals and colourful fish.

Situated on the western end of the pass between Ribbon Reefs #9 and #10, Pixie's Pinnacle is one of those premier dive sites which practically everyone in the diving industry has heard of. Nearly breaking the surface, the top of the reef is a small platform about 15 metres across and the walls plunge straight down to about 20 metres, sloping off to the sand at around 30 metres.

Regularly voted one of the top dive sites on the Great Barrier Reef, Pixie's Pinnacle is frequently included in 'best of the world' lists as well. With so much hype, it's easy to understand how expectations on a first visit could be high and it's equally easy to understand how some divers might initially be disappointed when they first jump in. The site is quite small and divers in a hurry could check out a bit of the bottom and then race around the whole pinnacle in less than five minutes. But like good food, Pixie's Pinnacle needs to be savoured and divers who take their time are amply rewarded.

The best way to dive Pixie's is to jump in and head straight down to around 30 metres and check out the big fans and soft coral trees. Large cod, eagle rays, manta rays and whitetip sharks can commonly be seen at these depths.

Once you've had a look around, it's time to begin a slow, spiralling ascent, winding your way around and around the pinnacle. Go slowly and stop often to check out the smaller animals.

The section between 20 and 30 metres is a slope encrusted in hard corals and decorated with soft corals, sea whips, the occasional black coral tree and sea fans which decrease in size as you ascend.

The end of the sloping area is marked by a large saddle at 14 metres which is stuffed full of fans, soft corals, sponges and hydroids, all of which overlay a heavy encrusting undergrowth. Slower swimming reef fish such as rock cod, hawkfish and butterflyfish, hide amongst the tangled mass and clouds of orange and purple anthias sometimes fill the gutter to overflowing. Occasionally, large trevally zoom through turning the gutter into a kaleidoscope of colour as the small fish scramble to avoid being eaten. But within seconds, everything settles down again.

The saddle is the beginning of the rest of the dive which is a vertical pinnacle, lumpy with encrusting hard corals and speckled with smaller fans, sea whips and featherstars in every conceivable colour. Being situated in the tidal flow area between two reefs, the pinnacle is

regularly washed by currents, creating an exceptionally healthy environment for encrusting corals, sponges, hydroids and algae which battle fiercely for every centimetre of space.

Riddling the sheer walls of the pinnacle are many small caves, ledges and overhangs—homes to a variety of fascinating tropical marine life. The walls are studded with a variety of anemones, each complete with colourful anemonefish. Nudibranch lovers will think they've died and gone to heaven with many, many species represented on Pixie's Pinnacle. Divers will be amazed at the macro life and underwater photographers will use up their film in a matter of seconds.

Tiny pipefish, sometimes no more than 3 centimetres long, can be found gently nosing around the soft corals, looking for tasty morsels. Small shrimp pepper the bommie, lurking in holes and hiding at the base of soft corals and fans. Larger, banded coral shrimp can be found under almost all of the ledges. As you wind your way around the bommie, check out each featherstar for commensal crabs and shrimp. They're usually the same colour as the featherstar and sometimes difficult to spot.

Practically every hole, ledge and indenture is a cleaning station and there's no shortage of colourful reef fish floating motionlessly, mesmerised as shrimp and small cleaner wrasses pick over them. Octopuses can often be seen taking a stroll over the corals, flowing from one refuge to another.

The fish life is as impressive as the invertebrate life. Look for leaf scorpionfish hiding in holes. These animals are territorial and can usually be found in the same spot, week after week. Beautiful red squirrel fish peer out from ledges. With such huge eyes, these animals are nocturnal and do most of their hunting at night. During the day, they're happy to just hover near protective ledges and overhangs.

TOP: A coral trout gets cleaned at one of the many cleaning stations.

CENTRE: Various species of nudibranch live at Pixie's Pinnacle.

LEFT: Anemonefish are prolific and easy to photograph.

Covering the entire pinnacle like a cloud of fairy floss are millions of anthias in hues of bright purple, pink and orange. Cruising through the anthias are majestic lionfish, better known in the United States as turkey fish, no doubt because of their feathery appendages. Angelfish, butterfly-fish and colourful damsels all crowd around the pinnacle, and schools of fusiliers flow over the reef like molten silver.

With so much to look at on the pinnacle, it's hard to tear yourself away from the little stuff, but make sure to spend a few minutes checking out the blue water adjacent to the pinnacle. Giant and blue trevally regularly cruise the area, along with mackerel and dogtooth tuna. Barracuda hang languidly off the pinnacle, and manta rays and eagle rays often swoop past. Sharks regularly patrol the open water, often just on the edge of visibility, and minke whales are frequently spotted at Pixie's Pinnacle during June and July when they are migrating.

But wait, there's more! Save some air and film for the top of the bommie which is worth a dive all by itself. Sometimes only 2 metres deep, depending on the tide, the top of the bommie is a colourful garden of close-cropped hard corals, home to hermit crabs, nudibranchs and other molluscs. Often, clouds of baitfish hang over the bommie and marauding packs of blue-fin trevally, mackerel and queen-fish regularly bolt through, causing the baitfish to streak off in every direction. It's a real fish-eat-fish world down there.

While you can dive Pixie's Pinnacle in a matter of minutes, it would take a lifetime to truly get to know it. There are many fabulous pinnacles on the Ribbon Reefs, such as Steve's Bommie and Temple of Doom, but Pixie's Pinnacle seems to have a bit of just about everything the Great Barrier Reef has to offer.

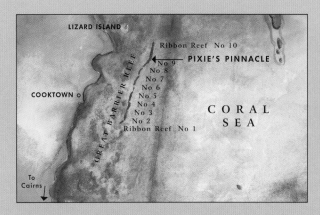

TRAVEL TIPS

GETTING THERE: 250 kilometres north of Cairns and 200 kilometres north of Port Douglas, Pixie's Pinnacle can only be dived via liveaboard charters.

BEST TIME TO GO: All year round.

CLIMATE: 21–31°C early summer through autumn (October–April), 18–26°C in winter through early spring (May–September). January and February are the warmest months. July and August are the coldest months. These temperatures are for Cairns; it will always be cooler at sea.

WATER TEMPERATURES: 27–29°C during October–March, most divers wear 3mm wetsuits. 24–26°C during April–September, most divers wear 5mm wetsuits.

VISIBILITY: 15–30 metres and variable.

SNORKELLING: Excellent.

OPERATORS

Just about any liveaboard which does the Ribbon Reefs will do Pixie's Pinnacle, including:

UNDERSEA EXPLORER (out of Port Douglas)
Tel: (07) 4099 5911, Fax: (07) 4099 5914
Email: undersea@ozemail.com.au
Internet: www.underseaexplorer.com

MIKE BALL DIVE EXPEDITIONS (out of Cairns)
Tel: (07) 4031 5484, Fax: (07) 4031 5470
Email: mbde@mikeball.com
Internet: www.mikeball.com

TAKA DIVE AUSTRALIA (out of Cairns)
Tel: (07) 4051 8722, Fax: (07) 4031 2739
Email: takadive@taka.com.au
Internet: www.taka.com.au

ABOVE: In only a few metres of water, at the top of Pixie's Pinnacle, blue-fin trevally race through a school of baitfish.

MINKE WHALES

ABOVE: A dwarf minke whale investigates both snorkellers and boat.

OPPOSITE: A pair of dwarf minke whales passes directly under a snorkeller.

Diving with whales is every diver's dream but most people go a whole lifetime without ever seeing one underwater. The reason is two-fold. In the first instance, whales don't usually frequent the areas preferred by divers, and secondly, many countries have enacted whale-protective legislation which prevents meaningful encounters. But on Queensland's northern Great Barrier Reef, snorkellers are legally allowed (under supervision) to have close, in-water encounters with dwarf minke whales.

Minke whales are small, by whale standards, reaching only around 11 metres in length and weighing a mere 9 to 10 tonnes. They can be found virtually worldwide, and most migrate seasonally from polar feeding grounds to warmer breeding grounds. Minke whales exist in good numbers and although they are not endangered, they are listed as a threatened species and are protected (since 1986) worldwide by international law. Some hunting still occurs under Japanese quota allowances for both consumption and scientific whaling.

Despite being the most common form of minke whale in the far northern Great Barrier Reef, the existence of a possible dwarf species of minke whale was only described in 1985. Although they have yet to be declared a separate species, this dwarf version is easily identified by a characteristic white patch extending from the shoulder to the base of its flipper. It also appears to be somewhat smaller than 'normal' minke whales, attaining an estimated maximum length of about 8 metres and 4 to 5 tonnes in weight. Like all minke whales, the dwarf minke whale exhibits an amazing curiosity, frequently approaching anchored or slow-moving vessels and even riding bow waves like very large dolphins.

Dwarf minke whale sightings are highly seasonal and 80 per cent occur in June and July when it is thought that some of these animals are migrating to cooler feeding grounds. During this five-week period, Australia's two most noted whale scientists, Dr Peter Arnold from the Museum of Tropical Queensland and Dr Alastair Birtles from James Cook University, co-host tourism/scientific expeditions with the *Undersea Explorer*, a liveaboard dive vessel well-known for the various innovative marine research projects it has pioneered.

Dwarf minke whale trips differ from normal liveaboard charters in both pace and the number of actual scuba dives. Your day usually begins with an early morning dive and then it's off

to look for minkes. Cruising slowly up and down transects which have been minke-rich on previous trips, the on-board scientists and their assistants never leave their posts on deck, constantly scanning the ocean for minke whales.

If a whale is sighted, the boat stops and drifts, while everyone holds a collective breath, preying that the whales will approach the boat. If they do, long, floating lines are set out from both bow and stern, and the research team quietly slips into the water to film the encounter, and hopefully identify a few of the animals. Once it has been established that the whales are going to stay with the boat for a while, guests, on snorkel, slip into the water and make their way to various stations along the floating lines, designated by knots, flags or even dangling, deflated tyre tubes.

Anxiously anticipating your first encounter, you twist and turn in the water, trying to look in all directions at once, usually flooding your snorkel in the process. Spotters standing on the top deck shout directions to the snorkellers and point to the various animals as they approach, giving the people in the water hints on which way to face.

Then, suddenly, a whale cruises into your vision, sometimes passing only a few metres underneath you in a seemingly endless parade of features. First there's a long, pointed snout, followed by a lopsided reverse grin and an inquisitive eye which registers complete awareness of your presence. A long, tapered body follows…and follows…and follows…punctuated finally by the unmistakable flukes of a whale's tail.

Seeing your first whale underwater is nothing short of a cosmic experience and few people can resist the temptation to try and communicate with them either by talking, singing or even mimicking their whale noises. It sounds silly but everyone does it, convinced that they

ABOVE: Encounters with minke whales are common during June and July.

OPPOSITE: Light rays converge on a pair of dwarf minkes.

are going to be the chosen ones...the ones to whom the whales pass on the secrets of the universe. Whales have this effect on humans.

Underwater encounters usually begin with one or two brave (or curious) animals doing lazy, loopy figures-of-eight underneath the boat, gliding slowly in and out of visibility as they scope the area. As their confidence increases, they approach the snorkellers, which seems to encourage shyer animals to move closer, too. Encounters usually last for over an hour as various individuals come and go. In one case, the *Undersea Explorer* reported almost 30 different animals in a single encounter which lasted almost eight hours. During the peak season, quality dwarf minke whale encounters are almost a sure thing, and in most cases, the boat breaks off the encounter after hours of interaction and data gathering.

Towards late afternoon, especially if the whales are being elusive, the boat will schedule another scuba dive. Still deep inside minke country, there's always a chance you will encounter a whale underwater. So keep a keen eye out towards the open water throughout your dive. Should you actually be approached by a dwarf minke whale while on scuba, simply hang quietly and let the animal approach you. Swimming towards the whale not only breaches regulations, but usually results in the animal leaving the area.

Between scuba dives and minke encounters, on-board scientists spend their time sifting through the data collected and conducting slide shows and briefings for the guests. As well as sharing their knowledge, the scientists are equally interested in collecting information from the guests regarding their individual experiences and any behaviour they may have witnessed. Research on dwarf minke whales is still in its infancy and nothing conclusive is known yet, regarding population size, breeding areas, spatial distribution, migration patterns or the significance of their behavioural antics. Every little piece of information helps.

Even vocalisations, so well documented in other species such as the humpback whale, are poorly understood. Up until a few years ago, many people believed dwarf minke whales were silent, but research carried out by a team of American scientists onboard the *Undersea Explorer* in 1997, recorded the first-known dwarf minke whale sounds (you can hear these recordings on the *Undersea Explorer's* web site). They are quite varied and range from low grunts to highly unusual, high-pitched, 'Star Wars'-style vocalisations.

From a diver's point of view, the most significant research carried out to date is the study proving that divers can have meaningful underwater encounters with dwarf minke whales without threatening the animals. The best

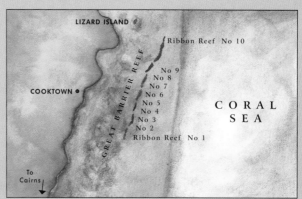

system seems to be using snorkel rather than scuba and remaining loosely grouped by the means of long floating lines. The lines are also safety devices, providing buoyancy and a firm connection to the boat which often drifts quite quickly in the strong winds usually associated with the dwarf minke whale season.

After years of restrictive legislation which virtually precluded any sort of meaningful in-water encounter with whales, the value of true eco-tourism, and the increased awareness which it fosters, is finally being recognised. The Code of Practice developed for dwarf minke whale tourism on the Great Barrier Reef is an example of the win-win result which can be reached when scientists, dive operators and government officials acknowledge the needs of all parties and work towards a solution which benefits everyone.

ABOVE: Scientist Alistair Birtles explains starfish physiology between sightings.

OPPOSITE LEFT: Ropes keep snorkellers grouped and attached to the boat.

OPPOSITE RIGHT: Minke whales are curious and come very close to drifting boats.

TRAVEL TIPS

GETTING THERE: Dwarf minke whales are accessible via liveaboard charter boats only.

BEST TIME TO GO: June and July.

CLIMATE: 18–24°C during June and July which are windy months. Pack a wind jacket and a track suit.

WATER TEMPERATURES: 24–26°C during June and July. Most divers wear 5mm wetsuits. Most snorkellers get cold floating for hours on the surface in the wind and many divers find thin neoprene vests and hoods useful.

VISIBILITY: 15–45+ metres.

SNORKELLING: All dwarf minke whale encounters are on snorkel. Ensure you have a good, hi-tech, splash-proof snorkel.

OPERATORS

Each operation runs dwarf minke whale charters differently. Some pursue minke whales seriously, reducing the number of scuba dives per day. Others approach it on a more opportunistic basis—if one is seen, then they will stop. Some feature celebrity scientists and some use spotter planes to locate the whales. Ask lots of questions before signing up for any trip to ensure your expectations will be met.

UNDERSEA EXPLORER (out of Port Douglas)
Tel: (07) 4099 5911, Fax: (07) 4099 5914
Email: undersea@ozemail.com.au
Internet: www.underseaexplorer.com

MIKE BALL DIVE EXPEDITIONS (out of Cairns)
Tel: (07) 4031 5484, Fax: (07) 4031 5470
Email: mbde@mikeball.com
Internet: www.mikeball.com

SCUBA ZOO

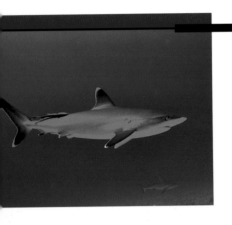

ABOVE: Silvertip sharks
are common at
Scuba Zoo.

OPPOSITE: Nothing can
beat a full-on shark
feeding frenzy.

The Coral Sea is known for its sharks which are so plentiful that most divers see at least one shark on virtually every dive. But once is never enough for divers, especially the more experienced ones, and exciting shark feeds rank highly on most divers' lists of 'must dos'.

Staged shark feeds are not permitted in the Great Barrier Reef itself, but the controlling authorities have no jurisdiction in the Coral Sea and most liveaboards cruising these outer areas put on some sort of shark feed for their guests. Some operators hand-feed wearing chain-mesh suits, some simply set bait out on the reef, some are pretty good and some are duds, but none of them come close to the heart-thumping action of Mike Ball's Scuba Zoo which is a full-on feeding frenzy.

Located on the western side of South Boomerang Reef in a sandy little bay only 15 metres deep are three permanently-moored shark cages. Made of aluminium amplimesh, they are 25 metres long in an L-shaped formation and comfortably hold 28 divers. Entry is from the back of the cages via a large gate which can be firmly closed and large viewing windows along the entire length of each cage give everyone (not just a few special photographers) a great, uninterrupted view of the action. A false floor keeps flapping fins off the bottom.

Arriving at the site, guests would never know that the sharks are already circling underneath the boat. Like Pavlov's dogs, they've learned over the years that boats mean food and some crew members believe that the sharks can actually recognise different boats.

Prior to gearing up, divers are given an in-depth shark brief which is part of Mike Ball's Reef Ecology Program. This enables divers to recognise common shark species and their behaviour patterns. They are shown video footage and slides on how the feed will proceed and how to best maximise fun and safety.

Jumping into the water as a group, divers make their way directly to the feeding area. Throughout the descent, divers will see many sharks. Some are already milling around the feeding area, others can be seen just on the edge of visibility. As the divers get closer to the feeding station, the sharks move in closer, too.

Prior to the formal feeding, divers are welcome to either enter the cages or lie on top of them and watch the sharks mill about. The first divemasters on the scene often rattle the chain on

the mooring block used for the bait. The sharks have learned to associate this noise with food and react instantly, moving in for a closer look every time they hear the rattle. It's hard to estimate numbers when there are so many and they're darting about so quickly, but it's safe to say that between 30 to 50 sharks show up for any given feed.

As more divers arrive and the chain is rattled again and again, the sharks become very alert and zip in and out of the feeding area. Divers lying on top of the cages can actually feel the sharks swimming over them, but they are not in any danger. Contrary to popular belief, sharks are not totally indiscriminant feeders, and Scuba Zoo sharks are only interested in the bait on the feeding mooring.

Once the divers are settled in their pre-feed positions either in or on top of the cage, a large metal rubbish bin full of bait is thrown off the boat and lowered slowly to the feeding area via a pulley system attached to a mooring located in front of the cages. The big splash as the can enters the water is the sharks' cue that the action is about to step up a level and the entire mob race to the surface. Caught many times on video, this phenomenon looks somewhat like a pyramid of sharks converging from a widespread area on the bottom to a single point on the surface, all in a matter of seconds.

The metal bin is perforated with large holes which help the can sink, but also allow the scent of the bait to escape, sending the sharks to higher levels of excitement. As it slowly sinks, dozens of sharks attack the bin, all intent on getting to the bait first and as the shark ball (kind of like a catfish ball but bigger) moves towards the feeding area, the action steps up yet another notch.

The actual feeding is over in a matter of minutes, so to prolong the fun, the crew hold off for about ten minutes, and just rattle the mooring chain periodically to renew the sharks' interest. Occasionally, they'll pull the bait can to within a couple of metres of the cage, which drags the shark ball to within metres of the divers and photographers, giving them a real up-close and toothy view.

Eventually, it's show time and divers are instructed to enter the cages and remove their fins, to help reduce silting. Once everyone is safely ensconced and the gates on the cages have been firmly shut, the lid of the bait can is removed (via a remote pulley) and the string of bait, attached to a buoy, pops out of the can. In a split second, a first-class frenzy is in progress. This is the real thing and divers will be glad they have the protection of the cages.

The large pieces of tuna are securely attached to the mooring and it takes a lot of effort for even a big shark to tear off a bite. The noise is amazing—you can actually hear the tuna being ripped to pieces. Once the food is gone, the sharks quickly lose interest. Many leave the area entirely; others continue to mill around in the distance, waiting to see if anything else is going to happen.

Eventually the 'all clear' is given, and divers are free to leave the cages and have a fossick around the mooring, looking for teeth which were dislodged during the frenzy. Sharks have rows of teeth. As the outer teeth wear and fall out, they are replaced with teeth from the next row. Losing teeth during feeding is normal for sharks.

As close to a sure thing as any shark dive can be, you'll see grey reef sharks, blacktip reef sharks, whitetip reef sharks and even silvertip sharks. Large hammerheads are less common but not unheard of.

OPPOSITE LEFT: The bait is brought to the site via a remote control pulley.

OPPOSITE RIGHT: Divers searching for shark teeth after the feeding frenzy is over.

BELOW: Whitetip reef sharks are curious and frequently approach divers at Scuba Zoo.

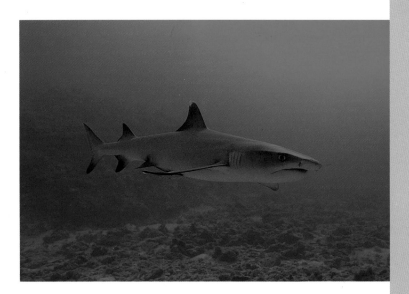

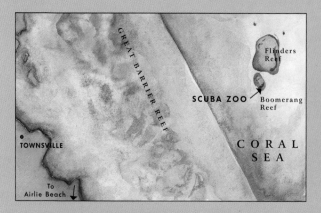

TRAVEL TIPS

GETTING THERE: An exclusive dive site operated by Mike Ball Dive Expeditions and located over 200 kilometres from Townsville, Scuba Zoo can only be dived via a Mike Ball Dive Expeditions Coral Sea liveaboard charter operating out of Townsville, Queensland.

BEST TIME TO GO: Scuba Zoo can be dived all year round. August through December has the least wind and rain.

CLIMATE: 21–31°C early summer through autumn (October–April), 17–26°C in winter through early spring (May–September). January and February are the warmest months. July and August are the coldest months. These temperatures are for Townsville; it will always be cooler at sea.

WATER TEMPERATURES: 25–28°C during October–March and most divers wear 3mm or 5mm wetsuits depending on how cold they get. 22–26°C during April–September and most divers wear 5mm wetsuits and sometimes hoods.

VISIBILITY: Visibility in the Coral Sea is excellent and reasonably consistent, averaging 25–35+ metres year round and often exceeding 60 metres. Visibility at Scuba Zoo is usually very good. The white sand bottom creates very bright conditions even on an overcast day.

SNORKELLING: Not recommended.

OPERATORS

MIKE BALL DIVE EXPEDITIONS
Tel: (07) 4031 5484, Fax: (07) 4031 5470
Email: mbde@mikeball.com
Internet: www.mikeball.com

FLINDERS REEF

ABOVE: Fans grow to amazing sizes in the Coral Sea.

OPPOSITE: A diver keeps pace with a passing hawksbill turtle.

Flinders Reef is a 1000 square kilometres coral reef located 220 kilometres north-east of Townsville, Queensland, deep in the Coral Sea. It is best described as a huge lagoon-type basin with a crescent-shaped reef in the south-east corner. Inside this massive lagoon, which is 5 kilometres deep in places, are hundreds of breathtaking pinnacles. Some nearly break the surface, while others are very deep. Some are so large that it seems as if they're separate reefs, offering a vast expanse of shallow diving on top in addition to their steep, plunging walls. Other pinnacles are so small on top that 20 divers seem like a crowd.

Only a two-hour cruise south-east from Flinders are North and South Boomerang reefs. These are offshoots of Flinders Reef and offer equally exciting dives, mainly on walls. The Boomerang Reefs don't offer any sheltered anchorages so are usually visited as day trips from Flinders, and for this reason, Flinders Reef and North and South Boomerang reefs are seen as a single destination. When divers refer to Flinders Reef, they usually mean these three reefs.

Diving Flinders is one of the world's truly exceptional diving experiences. The sheer, vertical walls go down forever. The fans are huge and the vibrant soft coral trees are the largest in the world. The pelagic action is incomparable, with huge schools of trevally, barracuda and snapper throughout the area. There are also rays, turtles and lots and lots of sharks.

And then there's the visibility! An average day presents 30–40 metres and 60+ metres is common all year round. Divers frequently report being able to read the name of the boat and count the number of people on the deco bar from a depth of over 30 metres. It's hard to get lost when you can see the boat from such a distance.

Flinders Reef is nitrogen overload and divers should both rest up and install fresh batteries in their dive computers before venturing to the Coral Sea. Typically, you'll start your day with a fairly deep dive to sample some of the outstanding fans and soft corals for which the area is so famous. The Cod Wall is home to 'Gigantus Gorgonus', a huge 4-metre-wide gorgonian fan sitting all by itself on a ledge in 36 metres of water. It's easy to find since you can usually see it from the surface. The first few divers to the ledge will often catch a glimpse of a giant hammerhead shark which frequents the area, but it is very shy and after quickly checking out the action, it usually departs.

At depth, have a good look at the fan, maybe peer over the edge of the ledge to see what's lurking in even deeper water and then start working your way back up the wall which is studded in a Flinders-typical cornucopia of thick encrusting corals, sponges, fans, sea whips, and colourful reef fish. On top of the Cod Wall are fissures which lead into a sandy basin, home to fan-choked gutters and coral-encrusted overhangs. This is a good place to just potter and off-gas at the end of a dive.

Other deep dives include a variety of sites offering spectacular soft corals. The Abyss, Midnight, Softwood Forest, Thermal Towers and Soft Spot all offer groves of huge soft coral trees at depths of 35–60 metres. Yes, that's deep, but the corals are absolutely spectacular. In a kaleidoscope of reds, yellows, deep purples and pastel mauves, these soft corals often achieve heights of 3 metres and have trunks as thick as your torso. The deeper you go, the bigger the soft coral trees.

After doing a couple of deep soft coral dives, you'll probably move on to the next big attraction at Flinders—the fish. There are several pinnacles in the lagoon which seem to be fish magnets. Usually these pinnacles are quite small on the top, sometimes no bigger than a house, and usually 10–18 metres at its shallowest point. Circling on top of these bommies are massive schools of trevally and barracuda which spend the day swirling and streaming. Packed in a tight circle, they'll swirl for a while, then break off, stream across to the other side of the bommie and regroup in another tight circle. Seemingly oblivious to the outside world, the fish rarely react even if divers move into the middle of the pack. It's an amazing experience to be surrounded by giant fish such as barracuda. Sometimes they're so dense that sunlight cannot penetrate through and the gloom inside the school can be a little disconcerting.

Sometimes the barracuda and trevally mix and sometimes they stay in separate groups. Sometimes they're right over the bommie, sometimes they're off to one side hovering in the open water. Closer to the reef are schools of mackerel, surgeonfish and fusiliers which streak over the reef like liquid mercury. Darting in and out are dogtooth tuna, and manta rays often make passing appearances. Usually on a mission, they appear, circle once or twice, and then head off into the big blue.

While the fish are great at these dive sites, don't overlook the pinnacles themselves which are usually encrusted in corals, sponges, bryozoans, nudibranchs and a variety of reef fish including lots of anemonefish. Although divers don't have to go deep, the call of the depths is difficult to

OPPOSITE LEFT: *Tiny porcelain crabs hide in anemones.*

OPPOSITE CENTRE: *Mating nudibranchs.*

OPPOSITE RIGHT: *Goby on a sponge.*

OPPOSITE BOTTOM: *Detail of soft coral found in deep water.*

LEFT: *Many pinnacles have resident schools of trevally.*

BELOW: *Some sites are virtually wall-to-wall anemonefish.*

resist and most people dip down a bit deeper for at least a few minutes just to check things out.

After a dive or two, it's probably time to ease up for the day and Flinders still has lots to offer. The tops of many of the bommies are quite shallow and feature beautiful marine gardens with untouched, colourful hard coral patches, home to hermit crabs, reef fish including parrotfish, lionfish and butterflyfish, and sometimes acres of anemonefish.

A trip to Flinders Reef always includes a stop (or two) at Flinders Cay, a permanent sand cay on the southern end of the reef. This area is protected and always calm, making it popular after a day of rocking and rolling in the wind. The cay itself is home to an automatic weather station and hundreds of seabirds which nest in certain seasons. Turtles use the area for nesting, and mating turtles are a common sight in the lagoon during summer months.

Underwater, there are clumps of coral outcrops scattered across the sand in no more than 12–18 metres. Pottering from one clump to the next, divers can find moray eels, coral trout, cardinalfish, nudibranchs, shrimps and colourful crabs. Stingrays often nestle in the sand under ledges and in large sandy patches, elusive garden eels undulate.

Night diving is excellent around Flinders either in the cay or on the bommies. On the sand flats, molluscs, including colourful but deadly cone shells, come out of hiding and

begin their nightly search for food. On the reefs, there's a complete change of guard when the sun goes down, and daytime animals are replaced by shrimp, decorator crabs, sea urchins, basket stars, squid and a variety of sleeping fish, including colourful parrotfish in their protective cocoons.

Flinders Reef is world-class diving but there is a cloud to every silver lining. Flinders is a long way from shore and it takes a fast boat over 12 hours to get there. The crossing can be choppy and few people sleep well the first and last night of the trip. During the windy season surface conditions can be rough even in the shelter of Flinders Reef, and riding a bucking boat all day is as tiring as the diving itself.

As the reef is made mostly of walls, divers can choose their depths, but the lure of the spectacular at extreme depths is hard to resist and is encouraged by the warm, clear water. Most divers find themselves popping down deeper at Flinders than they normally would elsewhere. It's some of the best diving in the world and by the end of the trip, everyone is nitrogen-enriched and exhausted. It's a great feeling.

ABOVE: Deep gutters are often packed with sea fans.

OPPOSITE: Flinders Reef is known for its fans and soft corals.

OVERLEAF: Sand cays offer respite from rough seas.

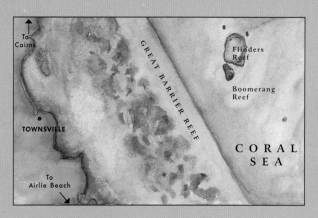

TRAVEL TIPS

GETTING THERE: Flinders and North and South Boomerang reefs can only be reached by live-aboard charter boats. Operators leave from both Townsville and Airlie Beach.

BEST TIME TO GO: The rainy season is in summer (January–March). The windy season is in winter (April–July). Diving is great all year round but the calmest, driest weather is between August and December.

CLIMATE: 21–31°C early summer through autumn (October–April), 17–26°C in winter through early spring (May–September). January and February are the warmest months. July and August are the coldest months. These temperatures are for Townsville; it will always be cooler at sea.

WATER TEMPERATURES: 25–28°C during October–March and most divers wear 3mm or 5mm wetsuits depending on how cold they get. 22–26°C during April–September and most divers wear 5mm wetsuits and sometimes hoods.

VISIBILITY: Visibility around Flinders Reef is excellent and averages 25–35+ metres year round, often exceeding 60 metres. It is some of the clearest water in the scuba diving world.

SNORKELLING: Many reefs have shallow areas providing excellent snorkelling. Conditions can be rough, especially during the windy season.

OPERATORS

MIKE BALL DIVE EXPEDITIONS (out of Townsville)
Tel: (07) 4031 5484, Fax: (07) 4031 5470
Email: mbde@mikeball.com
Internet: www.mikeball.com

MASS SPAWNING

ABOVE: A hard coral releases large gamete bundles.

OPPOSITE: A female Bohadschia graeffei releasing her eggs.

Not so much a specific dive site, the mass spawning on the Great Barrier Reef in Queensland is more of an Australian diving phenomenon. Corals reproduce in two ways: 1) asexually via budding, where polyps split, producing a second animal identical to the first, and 2) sexually, which is achieved by spawning and the subsequent union of egg and sperm.

For years it was believed that coral spawning was an all-year affair involving sperm from one colony drifting haphazardly through the ocean before stumbling onto and fertilising eggs from another colony of the same species. But in the early 1980s, scientists working on the Great Barrier Reef made a remarkable discovery.

Rather than being random and haphazard, the spawning of corals and many other invertebrates was actually a carefully orchestrated affair taking place over a consolidated period of eight nights following the full moon in either October or November. In what can only be described as a marine Mardi Gras, these eight nights are the setting for bizarre behaviour changes, bacchanal style excesses and frequent underwater snow storms.

Normally happy to crawl around on the sand for most of their lives, over the first few nights after the full moon, sea cucumbers begin a laborious migration, climbing to the very highest point on the reef. Not satisfied with the highest rock, particularly determined sea cucumbers elevate themselves even further by climbing up sea fans and even slender sea whip stalks.

Finally satisfied they can get no higher, they then rear up like cobras and begin swaying back and forth in the water column. Sea cucumbers eject their gametes through a tiny pore on the top of their heads which enlarges like an engorged pimple just prior to spawning. Males spawn slowly over a period of many minutes, oozing out a constant trickle of sperm as they wave their heads about, most likely in an attempt to disperse their genetic material as widely as possible. Female sea cucumbers are far less common than male sea cucumbers and their spawning behaviour is somewhat different. They, too, climb to high places and rear up like cobras, but the actual release of eggs is in one big puff which occurs only after nearly an hour of rearing and waving, interspersed with periods of rest.

Watching giant clams spawn is like watching grass grow. Unlike sea cucumbers, they don't give any outward signs that they're going to spawn and to witness it, you simply have to select

a clam and sit by it for as long as possible, hoping that it finally decides to do something before you run out of air. If you're lucky, it will suddenly contract several times and then forcefully shoot out a cloud of gametes reminiscent of a genie coming out of a bottle. On cue, once the first clam has gone, the others follow suit creating a domino effect of spawning clams right across the reef. Invariably, the next clam to spawn is always the one right behind you.

Plate corals and branching corals are the species primarily responsible for the underwater snow storms. Being hermaphrodites (both sexes in the same animal), these animals eject tightly-packed bundles of both eggs and sperm. Depending on the species, these bundles can be as small as the head of a pin or as big as a small peppercorn, and can range in colour from white to a variety of vibrant pinks, purples and reds. On cue, one specimen will begin a slow trickle of gamete bundles, but within seconds it's a full-on blizzard with all the other members of the same species spawning their little hearts out. Very quickly, the water becomes thick with tiny, colourful dots slowly rising to the surface where they will eventually break apart, allowing fertilisation to take place.

Not only do the corals go crazy but so do the fish, who explode into a feeding frenzy once the coral start spawning. All reason is abandoned and blinded either by divers' torches or perhaps by the feeding frenzy itself, many fish end up colliding into both the reef and nearby divers, which can

be a little disconcerting at night when divers' imaginations tend to run wild at the best of times.

Invertebrates also indulge in excesses. Small crabs position themselves amongst the branching tentacles of the spawning corals and stuff themselves to such extreme that they can hardly move, becoming prey to other animals such as small moray eels. Brittle stars sweep the spawning corals with their long feathery arms, entrapping the bundles in their sticky tentacles. Shellfish come out of the sand to feast, not only on entrapped gamete bundles, but also on the swarms of microscopic planktonic animals attracted to divers' torches.

The action is non-stop mid-water, too. On their own cues, worms begin reproducing and the water quickly fills with what looks like little worms but are actually reproductive segments of the worms. These are attracted to the lights of divers' torches, creating a tangled mass if a torch stays in one position for too long. They also tend to wiggle around divers' ears and can enter the outer ear. To prevent this, many divers wear lightweight lycra hoods on coral spawning nights.

On the surface, a slick begins to form as more and more gamete bundles arrive and unravel. This is fair game for a variety of surface dwelling fish such as garfish and flyingfish. Even jellyfish get into the act, using their tentacles like feather dusters to sweep through the gamete slick collecting up a feast which probably won't be matched until the same time next year.

Recreational divers can witness this amazing phenomenon via specially organised charters. Because there are so many different species all spawning at different times, it's important that a scientist travels with the group to coordinate the diving. Each day, guests are presented with briefings and slide shows, highlighting those species likely to spawn that evening and what time they are expected to 'go off'. Before the sun sets, divers normally do a recognisance dive to map the area under the boat, highlighting the location of targeted species. Shallow reefs are always chosen to maximise bottom times.

Once the sun sets, it's time to begin the long underwater vigil. Rather than just sitting in one place, eventually freezing to death, spend your dive slowly swimming a circuit which passes by the animals you scouted out earlier in the day. Look for unusual or erratic behaviour, such as sea cucumbers in places they shouldn't be or overly active fish. Also, keep your eyes peeled for other species which might be spawning, including worms and anemones.

Witnessing a mass spawning could easily be the most exhausting diving you're ever likely to do. Not only do you spend hours in the water every night, but you have to do a few dives each day in preparation for the ensuing night's activities. Sometimes you'll spend a whole night and see nothing…or very little. But on other nights, it seems to all happen at once. Kneeling on the sand, dopey from sleep deprivation, watching a plate coral go off and knowing that the exact same thing is happening over an area of many square kilometres is both awe-inspiring and humbling. Witnessing this amazing event is one of diving's special experiences.

OPPOSITE LEFT: Some corals release gamete bundles in unison.

OPPOSITE CENTRE: Spawning sea anemones are rarely seen.

OPPOSITE RIGHT: Gamete bundles are eaten by many animals.

TRAVEL TIPS

GETTING THERE: Mass spawning occurs throughout the Great Barrier Reef, and boats depart from any number of Queensland towns.

BEST TIME TO GO: Varies. Generally, spawning occurs during the week following the full moon in either October or November.

CLIMATE: Early spring (October–November) and air temperatures in Townsville average 21–31°C.

WATER TEMPERATURES: 24–27°C for the middle reef area. Southern reefs could be colder and northern reefs could be slightly warmer. Most divers wear 3mm or 5mm wetsuits. Some divers wear a thin neoprene vest and a light hood for added warmth on long night dives.

VISIBILITY: Visibility throughout the Great Barrier Reef averages 15–25 metres and fluctuates a great deal.

SNORKELLING: Most spawning takes place at night and is best witnessed using scuba.

OPERATORS

Some charters treat spawning trips casually, hoping that they will stumble across some activity on a scheduled night dive. Other charters take spawning trips seriously. Ask plenty of questions when booking.

UNDERSEA EXPLORER (out of Port Douglas)
Tel: (07) 4099 5911, Fax: (07) 4099 5914
Email: undersea@ozemail.com.au
Internet: www.underseaexplorer.com

MIKE BALL DIVE EXPEDITIONS (operates out of Cairns and Townsville)
Tel: (07) 4772 3022, Fax: (07) 4721 2152
Email: mbde@mikeball.com
Internet: www.mikeball.com

THE WRECK OF THE SS YONGALA

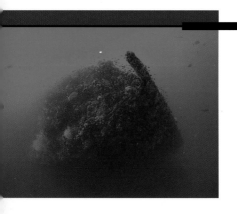

ABOVE: Still intact, the bow of the SS Yongala looms up from the depths.

OPPOSITE: The aft samson-posts are encrusted with invertebrate life.

The SS *Yongala* was a passenger and cargo ship built in 1903 in Newcastle-on-Tyne in England, on behalf of the Adelaide Steamship Company. Considered by one and all to be a very handsome ship, it was 110 metres long and provided accommodation for 110 first-class passengers and about 130 second-class passengers.

No expense was spared when building the SS *Yongala*, with special attention paid to ventilating the ship. Powerful fans pumped fresh air throughout the living areas via dedicated ducts. It was also fitted throughout with yet another luxury—electric lights, complete with their own special-purpose generator.

The *Yongala* was first assigned to a Sydney–Fremantle route catering to the booming gold rush business, but as trade waned, Queensland was added to its route, including a Melbourne–Cairns run, which proved to be so popular that it ended up spending most of its time on this route.

The SS *Yongala's* voyage between Melbourne and Cairns in late March 1911 began routinely and it worked its way up the coast, dropping off and picking up passengers and cargo as it went, without incident. On Thursday, 23 March, the *Yongala* departed a Queensland island for the final 335 kilometres to Townsville.

Threatening skies and moderate breezes quickly developed into heavy rains, wind, squalls, and rough seas. There was even a formal cyclone warning between Mackay and Townsville. Visibility was reduced to practically zero and probably the furthest the captain could see was the white water immediately surrounding the vessel. Battling the elements, the SS *Yongala* was last seen passing the Dent Island Lighthouse about 6.30pm that evening.

No-one knows exactly what happened to the *Yongala*. Perhaps it rode down the crest of a giant wave and broached, or possibly, it was rolled by a cross sea and did not have time to recover before it was struck by another wave. At first its delayed arrival created little concern as it was assumed it had moved out to sea to ride out the storm, but when it still had not arrived almost 24 hours later, the alarm was raised and one of Australia's most intensive sea searches was put into action.

Despite meticulous searching in the surrounding seas, along the coastline and the inner fringes of the Great Barrier Reef, no evidence of the *Yongala's* demise was ever found. Five days

after its disappearance, though, flotsam began washing ashore as far as 80 kilometres from Townsville, including a unique lettered door which had stood between the music room and promenade deck of the *Yongala*.

The disappearance of the *Yongala* and its 121 passengers and crew proved to be an intriguing mystery. What route did it take through coastal islands? Did it strike a reef or just turn turtle in the cyclonic seas? The vessel was never really forgotten as the years passed, especially in Queensland, and its mysterious disappearance often appeared as historical features in newspapers and magazines throughout Australia.

In 1943, during the war years, mine-sweepers clearing the shipping lanes off Queensland came across an obstruction off Cape Bowling Green which they entered onto their charts as a shoal. It was subsequently forgotten until after the war. In 1947 sweeps of the area using anti-submarine instruments and echo sounders concluded that this 'shoal' was actually a shipwreck approximately 100 metres long. Speculation rose, but it wasn't until 1958 that the wreck was positively located and dived by helmet divers (at that time, scuba equipment was still in experimental stages). Identifying the wreck was easy as the word 'Yongala' was plastered along the bow in 30-centimetre-high brass letters.

Today, the SS *Yongala* is a famous tourist attraction, visited by many scuba divers every week. Located in the middle of a shipping lane only 24 kilometres from shore, boats pick up moorings placed around the wreck and divers follow descent lines to the bottom. The *Yongala* rests on its

starboard side, with the deepest point being 33 metres under the bow. The port edge of the top deck rests in only 15 metres of water.

The *Yongala* is rarely an easy dive. The water is usually murky, surface conditions are generally rough, and strong, cross-beam currents are common. Jumping off a crashing boat and hanging onto a descent line for dear life makes for a dramatic descent, but things settle down somewhat once you're on the bottom, since there is always a lee side to the current.

Descending towards the *Yongala* is impressive. Before you see the wreck, you'll pass through several layers of fish. The first layer is a school of friendly batfish which quickly congregate near the surface when a charter boat arrives, looking for handouts. Some are so tame you can hand feed them and virtually lift them out of the water. Descending further into the gloom, you'll pass by impressive pelagics such as kingfish, trevally and barracuda.

The first sight of the wreck is equally impressive. Virtually intact, this is not just a pile of wreckage. The bow still looms out over the sand. Rusting davits stand mutely, silhouetted against the blue emptiness. Gaping black holes open into the holds, and the big brass letters spelling out 'Yongala' are still visible courtesy of regular polishing by visiting divemasters.

OPPOSITE: Colourful corals encrust the vessel's superstructure.

BELOW: Painted sweetlips hover under the stern of the SS Yongala.

After almost a century, the *Yongala* is carpeted in a thick marine growth of algae, sponges, hard and soft corals, hydroids and sea whips. Passing stingrays and manta rays are common, as are shark sightings.

Scattered on the sand, amongst piles and piles of oyster shells, is a variety of wreckage including toilet bowls, dinner plates, bed frames and drainage grates. The *Yongala* is protected under the *Queensland Historic Shipwrecks Act* and nothing can be removed from the wreck. Nor can divers penetrate the wreck, both for safety as well as problems associated with accelerated deterioration caused by trapped air pockets.

Despite being unable to penetrate the wreck, there's still plenty to see on the decks and adjacent sand and it is easy to circumnavigate the entire wreck on one dive. Large cod rest in the murky recesses under the bow and a school of sweetlip almost always congregates under the stern. The holds are filled with millions of cardinalfish which dart back and forth in unison when trevally and kingfish race through looking for a feed.

Every inch of the hull is covered in exceptionally thick and colourful growth. Reef fish such as angelfish and coral trout hover amongst the growth along with larger animals such as turtles which can often be seen napping in the thick growth or wedged under the hull.

During certain seasons the entire area crawls with olive sea snakes. Although poisonous, olive sea snakes are not aggressive and don't attack. Sometimes they're curious though, and will move in for a closer look. In these cases, just stay calm and they'll move on.

As scuba diving sites go, the SS *Yongala* is just about as exciting as it gets, particularly if you like to see lots of large fish and lush carpets of sponges and corals. But it can be a difficult and daunting dive. Many charters feature a visit to the SS *Yongala* as part of a longer trip to the Coral Sea and many, many charters have to cancel the visit to the *Yongala* due to bad surface conditions. There are the occasional calm days on the *Yongala* but they can only be considered a gift.

Jumping off the back of a boat, desperately trying to grab the descent line before being swept out to sea and clinging to it as you descend could deter the faint-hearted. But for those who persevere, the rewards are great. Many consider the SS *Yongala* one of the world's top dive sites.

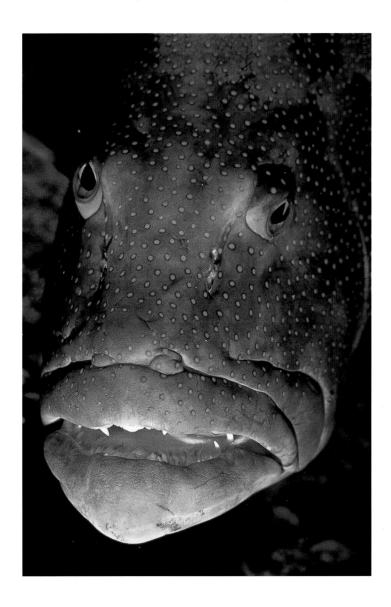

ABOVE: Large coral cod lurk in murky holds.

OPPOSITE TOP: The wreck is covered with encrusting growth.

OPPOSITE CENTRE: Cup coral polyps closed during the day.

OPPOSITE BOTTOM: Cup coral polyps opened at night.

TRAVEL TIPS

HOW TO GET THERE: Operators leave from either Townsville or Airlie Beach.

BEST TIME TO GO: The least windy period is early spring through summer (September–March). Of that period, September through December has the least rain and the best visibility.

CLIMATE: Summer (October–March) ranges from 20–33°C. December and January are the warmest months. Winter (April–September) ranges from 14–25°C. July and August are the coldest months.

WATER TEMPERATURES: 23–28°C in summer, with January, February and March averaging 28°C. Divers usually wear 3mm steamers or 5mm suits if they're prone to cold. 22–25°C in winter with July and August averaging 22°C. Most divers wear two-piece 5mm wetsuits and sometimes hoods.

VISIBILITY: Visibility on the wreck is usually murky, averaging only about 15 metres.

SNORKELLING: Not recommended.

OPERATORS

Most boats operating out of Townsville and Airlie Beach, visit the *Yongala* as part of a liveaboard trip to the Great Barrier Reef and Coral Sea.

MIKE BALL DIVE EXPEDITIONS (out of Townsville)
Tel: (07) 4031 5484, Fax: (07) 4031 5470
Email: mbde@mikeball.com
Internet: www.mikeball.com

PRO DIVE TOWNSVILLE
Tel: (07) 4721 1760, Fax: (07) 4721 1760
Email: prodivet@ultra.net.au
Internet: http://ultra.ultra.net.ay/~prodivet/home.html

THE SOLITARY ISLANDS

ABOVE: North Solitary
Island is home to
temperate-tropical diving.

OPPOSITE: Giant cuttlefish
are prolific in winter
when they breed.

Coffs Harbour is a thriving tourist town on the mid-north coast of New South Wales, 750 kilometres north of Sydney and 430 kilometres south of Brisbane. A Mecca for holiday makers, Coffs Harbour offers funky tourist attractions such as wooden clog factories, miniature golf, water slides and, of course, the Big Banana, the world's largest fibreglass banana.

Radiating inland from Coffs is beautiful country with lush banana plantations, rainforests and rolling foothills leading into the Great Dividing Range. There are tracks for four-wheel-drive vehicles and well-manicured, sign-posted hiking trails through many of the rainforests, some leading to secluded waterfalls. Such beautiful, unspoiled countryside is a natural magnet to creative people and the surrounding hills are home to a thriving artist's community ranging from painting and pottery to furniture making.

Australians love the water and Coffs Harbour delivers. There are many kilometres of abandoned beaches offering secluded sunbaking, swimming, surfing, fishing and, in certain areas, four-wheel-driving on the beaches.

Adjacent to Coffs Harbour lies the Solitary Islands Marine Park. Spanning roughly 70 kilometres of coastline beginning slightly south of Coffs Harbour and working northwards to Plover Island, the whole area is bathed in a unique mix of tropical and temperate currents unlike anything else on Australia's eastern coastline. The result is a fascinating mix of marine communities. Tropical species from the Great Barrier Reef, such as corals and reef fish, live cheek by jowl with temperate species, such as morwong, kingfish, groper and jewfish.

The Solitary Islands are recognised as the southern-most limit of many reef building corals on Australia's eastern coastline, and while not nearly as big as in the Great Barrier Reef, the corals surrounding the Solitary Islands are well established and healthy, allowing many tropical species to flourish.

The Solitary Islands can be divided roughly into two areas, North and South. The South Solitaries are made up of five islands/shoals, three pinnacles and some shallow-water reefs, and due to proximity, are normally serviced by dive operators located in Coffs Harbour itself. The South Solitaries offer dramatic underwater terrain such as valleys, gutters, caves and peaks. Some dives feature avalanches of large boulders tumbling down into the depths and

LEFT: Manta rays cruise the islands from January to March.

BELOW: Leopard sharks are common in the summer months.

OPPOSITE: Deep gutters are often filled with tiny baitfish.

there are even a few small kelp forests, home to crustaceans and juvenile fish.

The North Solitary Islands consist of one small island, two larger ones and a number of reefs and pinnacles. Located further north, the North Solitaries are totally different to the South Solitaries. They are surrounded by much deeper waters, and being further offshore, they are regularly bathed in cleaner, bluer currents. While the South Solitaries can be described as temperate diving with dashes of tropical, the North Solitaries are more tropical with dashes of temperate animals.

The North Solitary Islands are serviced primarily by dive operators located north of Coffs Harbour in coastal towns such as Mullaway which is only a few kilometres north of Coffs. There are no boat ramps near Mullaway and launching takes place on a large, flat, hard-sand beach off Arrawarra Headland. The tractors used to launch the boats are frequently backed well into the water. They don't last very long.

The jewel of the Solitary Islands is without a doubt North Solitary Island, and Anemone Bay is a 'must do' site located on the north end of North Solitary Island. Sheltered from strong southerly seas, this small bay has a barren rocky bottom smothered in anemones and

anemonefish. The quantity, which many consider to be one of the densest aggregations in the world, is difficult to imagine until witnessed. During dive briefings, first-timers often ask for further details on how to find the anemones, not realising that they are literally everywhere.

But Anemone Bay is more than just anemones. Circling in the mouth of the bay are small squadrons of eagle rays, and in spring and early summer, manta rays are practically a sure thing. Small schools of barracuda are also common. Along the east wall are amazing cleaning stations where huge surgeonfish, goatfish and red morwong float in trances as cleaner wrasse pick over them. Colourful schools of striped snapper also congregate in the bay.

On the west side of Anemone Bay are gutters where leopard sharks and more manta rays can be found. Further out in slightly deeper waters, grey nurse and whaler sharks

are common. Don't forget to look up when off the west point. Large schools of trevally frequently circle slightly outside of the bay in the current.

Further around the west point are slopes and gutters. The gutters aren't very deep and a few minutes fossicking under the rocky rubble almost always produces interesting nudibranchs, hermit crabs and exquisite little boxer crabs which fight off predators many times larger than themselves with little anemones they hold in their front claws. The small caves regularly produce grey nurse sharks in winter and the occasional tropical whitetip reef shark in the summer. The entire area is littered with *Ovula* cowries, predominantly the black-mantled *ovum*, but also the golden-mantled *costellata*.

One great dive site simply isn't enough and North Island has more to offer than Anemone Bay. On the west side of the island, divers can explore bubble caves, canyons, gutters and swim-throughs. Many of the gutters cut deeply

into the island, ending in narrow crevices and caves often filled with thousands of tiny, silver baitfish. Watch your hands and feet in these areas as large wobbegong sharks often rest motionlessly under the baitfish, waiting in ambush for an unsuspecting tasty morsel to blunder by.

North West Rock is only a hop from North Solitary Island and is frequently visited as the second dive of the day. Picking up a mooring in a secluded bay on the west side, divers swim through a narrow slot to a dive site called Fish Soup on the east side. The area is aptly named and the entire eastern wall is usually covered in schools of morwong, snapper, surgeonfish, rabbitfish and mullet. Tucked in amongst the boulders are pockets of golden bullseyes. Ever-present wobbegongs drape themselves over rocks and under ledges, and the whole area is encrusted in temperate and tropical invertebrates such as small fans, ascidians, bryozoans and nudibranchs, including large Spanish dancers.

Towards the end of the dive, swim back through the slot to the western side and potter in the protected bay where there are more anemonefish and cowries. In the shallows are large clumps of branching staghorn coral, home to juvenile tropical fish, and under ledges divers can often find slumbering hawksbill turtles. Don't forget to look overhead for yet more mantas and leopard sharks.

Closer to shore is North West Solitary Island, home to excellent snorkelling and magnificent black coral trees. The whole area is encrusted with corals and sponges, and nudibranchs are common. Hovering over the reef, divers

frequently encounter giant cuttlefish in winter months and under ledges one can find colourful blue devils and tropical rock cods all year round.

Not for the faint of heart is a dive on the east side of North West Solitary Island called Misty Valley. Only accessible on calm days, gutters run the length of the island. Swimming through the gutters, divers must stay close to the bottom and remain negatively buoyant. Every few minutes a wave crashes over the ledge, filling the gutters with bubbles which roll down the slope towards the divers like a fog rolling down a mountainside. When the mist engulfs you, visibility is reduced to zero for several seconds and all you can do is wait for the bubbles to clear before moving on.

The trick on this dive is to move slowly, stop often and look up. Frolicking in the white water above you are schools of fish and even turtles, seemingly unperturbed by the turbulence which periodically crashes down on them.

The Solitary Islands are a perfect mix of equally exciting temperate and tropical marine life and the northern islands, being bathed regularly in clear, blue currents, are very special diving indeed.

ABOVE: A colourful mantis shrimp strolls across the sand.

OPPOSITE TOP: Golden-mantled costellata *feeding on a sponge.*

OPPOSITE BOTTOM: Boxer crabs hold anemones in their claws.

TRAVEL TIPS

GETTING THERE: Coffs Harbour has a regional airport with daily flights from Sydney and Brisbane.

BEST TIME TO GO: All year round. Grey nurse sharks and giant cuttlefish are prolific during July–August. Manta rays between January–March.

CLIMATE: 19–27°C during November–March, 10–20°C during April–September.

WATER TEMPERATURES: 20–25°C in the summer and most divers wear 5mm wetsuits or long johns. 18–21°C in winter and most divers wear 5mm two-piece wetsuits plus hoods during the coldest months.

VISIBILITY: 5–40+ metres. December–March offers good visibility. June–August averages 20 metres.

SNORKELLING: Excellent.

OPERATORS

Officially, most operators visit all islands, but in reality, Coffs Harbour operators visit the southern islands and operators further north visit the northern islands.

DIVE QUEST (northern operator, Mullaway)
Tel: (02) 6654 1930, Fax: (02) 6654 0328
Email: divequest@hot.net.au
Internet: www.divequest.com.au

JETTY DIVE CENTRE (southern operator, Coffs Harbour)
Tel: (02) 6651 1611, Fax: (02) 6652 5702
Email: dive@jettydive.com.au
Internet: www.jettydive.com.au

ABOVE: Fish Soup, on the eastern side of North West Rock, is thick with schooling fish.

SOUTH WEST ROCKS

ABOVE: Grey nurse sharks are common for most of the year.

OPPOSITE: The shallow end of Fish Rock Cave is fringed by sea fans.

South West Rocks is a coastal resort village situated in New South Wales, 480 kilometres north of Sydney and 510 kilometres south of Brisbane. The area is well known for its miles of beautiful beaches and impressive granite headlands, where tourists can watch dolphins frolic and whales migrate. Tourists flock to South West Rocks to relax, sunbake, fish and sightsee. Divers flock to South West Rocks for a single rocky outcrop called Fish Rock.

Fish Rock is a small, barren island located 3 kilometres offshore. Home to a few seabirds, the rocky cliffs tower 20 metres into the sky and plunge into the sea creating a similar underwater terrain. Surrounding the rock is an array of sites including gutters, walls, pinnacles, caves, tunnels and colourful sponge gardens. Located only 4 kilometres from the edge of the continental shelf, Fish Rock is home to an incredible number of fish, including lots of sharks.

Fish Rock Cave runs right through the island. Beginning at the deep end at 24 metres, the cave is narrow for the first 15 metres ending in a vertical chimney. Swim up the short chimney to the main chamber, and from there on, it's a straight shoot through to the other end. As it is almost 100 metres long, you cannot see light when you first enter the main chamber, but you can't get lost and as you slowly swim along, inspecting the walls, light from the other end eventually appears as a faint glow. The floor of the main chamber is rocky and the walls are covered in encrusting sponges of every imaginable colour, and speckled with orange cup corals, bryozoa, colonial ascidians, hydroids, nudibranchs and starfish. Tucked into the ledges are banded coral shrimp, slipper lobsters and many crayfish.

Schools of bullseyes and small baitfish swarm throughout the main chamber, sometimes blocking off visibility altogether. Should you decide to land on the bottom, watch your hands and feet as wobbegongs frequently rest in the cave.

Approaching the shallow entrance (at 10 metres), there are several bubble caves in the ceiling where divers can surface. There isn't usually a lot of surge in the cave, but on rough days, dramatic increases and decreases of pressure can be felt as the surge pumps back and forth. Dive computers go crazy in these conditions, reading the quick drops in pressure as fast ascents. In the bubble caves, the air sometimes rhythmically fogs and clears as sudden increases and decreases in pressure causes moisture in the air to mist over and then clear up.

The shallow end of the tunnel opens out into a huge cavern. With more light penetrating the area, the encrusting invertebrate growth is even more spectacular. The walls are studded with beautiful gorgonian fans, often home to interesting bubble shells and other small molluscs. Check out the corners for an old loggerhead turtle and inspect the walls and ceiling for tropical species such as lionfish and several species of tropical butterflyfish, which frequently get swept down from warmer waters further north.

Just outside of the shallow entrance is a large bowl called The Aquarium, home to huge quantities of fish. Look carefully among the rocks on the bottom for several varieties of moray eels including the beautiful mosaic moray.

Traversing Fish Rock Cave does not take long, so go slowly and have a good look at the walls and ceiling as you move through. Yes, it is dark in one section and the tunnels are small, but there is no risk of getting entangled or stuck. It's not that small. The boat operators give good briefings and most first-time visitors can successfully navigate it on their own. If for any reason you are unsure, the guides are always keen to conduct tours—any reason to get wet!

Along the southern side of Fish Rock is another great dive site called the Shark Gutters. A series of rocky ridges separated by sandy gutters run in a south-easterly direction from the island. Gradually getting deeper and deeper, the tops of the ridges run from 7 metres to 24 metres. The depth of the gutters run from 24 metres to 30 metres. In winter and spring, grey nurse sharks cruise these gutters, swimming lazily back and forth. On arrival, take a few minutes to rest on top of the ridges and simply watch the sharks as they cruise back and forth. Then descend into the gutter and slowly edge closer, hugging the walls to avoid spooking the sharks. Divers can often get quite close as long as they avoid jerky movements and stay close to the bottom.

The sharks are great, but take some time to inspect the walls of these gutters which feature excellent sponge growth including all the associated invertebrates which usually go along with healthy temperate water sponge gardens. Look for tiny cuttlefish hovering near sponges and colourful nudibranchs grazing through the encrusting algae.

In deeper waters, you will find large, black coral trees, which actually look white or beige. The coral skeleton is black but the live polyps are white. Inspect them closely for brilliant red snake stars, pygmy leatherjackets, juvenile fish and even the occasional long-nosed hawkfish, another species which sometimes gets swept south in warm currents.

Keep an eye out for wobbegongs in these gutters, along with stingrays, blue gropers and turtles. You can also find several large Queensland groper, and sometimes the yellowtail are so thick that you can't see your buddy. One old loggerhead turtle, possibly the same one which is frequently seen in the shallow end of Fish Rock Cave, often follows divers. For years it has been fed by divers, and local divers always bring along bits of fish or cunjevoi for the old thing.

On the north-east corner of Fish Rock is a twin-peaked sea mount, rising from around 35 metres up to a mere 6 metres under the surface, called the Pinnacles. This area is best known for its huge schools of fish. Spanish mackerel swirl the peaks along with yellowtail, pomfrets and silver sweep. Bonito rocket through on occasion, and often divers will encounter large schools of long-finned bannerfish, a phenomenon normally restricted to more tropical waters.

The Pinnacles is also wobbegong city and divers can often find dozens of them on this site, draped over rocks like Salvador Dali's melting clocks. Cruising through the area, mainly in the deeper gutters between the Pinnacles and the main island, are the ever-present grey nurse sharks.

Divers flock to the Pinnacles for the large numbers of fish, but take some time to inspect the more sedentary life. Hugging the rocks are red morwong, various wrasse, lionfish and surgeonfish which like to pick through the encrusting algae. There are also purple and pink sea tulips, colourful starfish, colonial ascidians, nudibranchs and bryozoa which often play host to *pycnogonids* or sea spiders.

One of the best single sites in New South Wales, Fish Rock offers unsurpassed fish life with huge dollops of sharks. The encrusting growth is thick and colourful and the terrain itself is well worth a visit. Fit divers, who are good on air, can swim completely around Fish Rock on a single dive. The less ambitious will prefer swimming off on the many tangents over a terrain which allows easy backtracking and little fear of getting lost. But best of all is the excitement of swimming through the island from one end to the other.

OPPOSITE LEFT: Colourful nudibranchs can be found throughout the Fish Rock area.

OPPOSITE CENTRE: A small moray eel peeps out from a bed of cup corals.

OPPOSITE RIGHT: A Spanish dancer crawls through thick invertebrate growth.

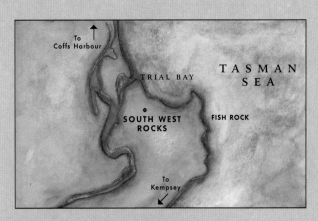

TRAVEL TIPS

GETTING THERE: The closest regional airport is Kempsey. You will need a car to get around.

BEST TIME TO GO: South West Rocks can be dived year round. The clearest water is during summer to early winter (January–May). The sharks are present from May to February.

CLIMATE: 17–29°C in spring and summer (November–March), 8–22°C autumn and winter (April–September).

WATER TEMPERATURES: Summer through autumn (January–April) averages 24–26°C. Winter ranges from 18–20°C. The coldest months are July and August. The warmest months are February and March. Most divers wear two-piece 5mm wetsuits in winter and remove the jackets for the warmer months.

VISIBILITY: From January to June, visibility averages 24 metres and often exceeds 30 metres. From July through December, visibility averages 15 metres.

SNORKELLING: Snorkelling around Fish Rock can be good on calm days. Always beware of currents.

OPERATORS

FISH ROCK DIVE CENTRE
Tel: (02) 6566 6614, Fax: (02) 6566 5585
Email: enquiries@fishrock.com.au
Internet: www.fishrock.com.au

SOUTH WEST ROCKS DIVE CENTRE
Tel: (02) 6566 6474, Fax: (02) 6566 6959
Email: info@southwestrocksdive.com.au
Internet: www.southwestrocksdive.com.au

SEAL ROCKS

ABOVE: The island at the end of Seal Rocks beach offers good snorkelling.

OPPOSITE: Snorkelling in a rock pool on an island off Seal Rocks Beach.

Technically, Seal Rocks is a collection of rocky outcrops just off the coastline of New South Wales, 290 kilometres north of Sydney, but most divers use the term 'Seal Rocks' collectively to refer to the whole dive destination adjacent to the twin regional towns of Forster and Tuncurry.

Seal Rocks is best known for its permanent colony of grey nurse sharks (*Carcharias taurus*) which are members of the sand tiger family of sharks, Odontaspididae. They are the sharks most frequently seen in large aquariums around Australia. Although grey nurse sharks are big, with lots of pointy teeth and sinister-looking little eyes, they are harmless to humans and only four occurrences of grey nurse sharks biting humans have ever been recorded. In each case, it was when divers were feeding the sharks in aquariums.

Grey nurse sharks are common up and down the New South Wales coastline where they migrate as water temperatures change. Preferring slightly colder waters, they usually head south in summer and back north when the water starts to cool down. Perhaps it's just the right mix of water temperatures, but for whatever reason, a permanent colony of grey nurse sharks has established itself in the general vicinity of Seal Rocks, and for years divers have been visiting the area specifically to see the sharks.

Big Seal Rock is a rocky outcrop located adjacent to a remote, isolated bush community, also called Seal Rocks (yes, it gets a little confusing!) The eastern side of 'Big Seal' features a vertical wall starting in 4 metres of water and plunging down to over 40 metres. The walls are thickly encrusted with temperate water invertebrates including sponges, sea tulips, colonial ascidians, starfish, bryozoa and brilliant red sea fans. Patrolling the walls are trevally, kingfish, mackerel and yellowtail, plus the occasional grey nurse shark.

But most divers head straight to the western side to a site called 'The Shark Gutters'. Anchoring in a tiny alcove which gives some protection from the wind, jump in and head towards the island. Leap frog over a few small gutters until you reach an unmistakably large gutter lined with rocks and crushed shells. Stop for a few minutes on the ridge above the gutter and watch the sharks peacefully traversing the gutter, moving from the open ocean up to a small amphitheatre and cave cut deeply into the island. The sharks tend to mill around in the amphitheatre.

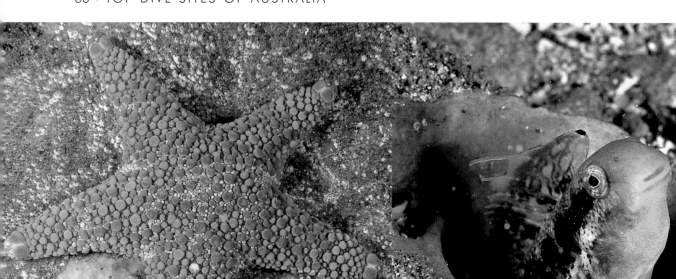

ABOVE LEFT: Firebrick sea stars cling to the walls of gutters and pinnacles.

ABOVE RIGHT: A small blennie protects eggs laid in an empty shell.

Leaving the ridge, stay close to the bottom and swim up one side of the gutter to the amphitheatre. You'll know when you've arrived because there will be a couple dozen sharks swimming in slow, lazy circles. Rather than actually entering the amphitheatre, stay low and rest on the bottom just on the edge. The sharks will cruise by within centimetres of you.

Keep an eye out as you edge along the gutter for napping wobbegongs, a species known to strike out if a hand or foot is placed too close to their heads. They may look docile and lethargic but they're not! Also look for turtles snoozing in the far corners. Don't forget to look up, too. Schools of kingfish, drummer and trevally can often be seen circling overhead.

Seal Rocks has other exciting dives, all featuring good pelagic action and colourful temperate water invertebrate growth. The Pinnacles is a group of underwater needles beginning in 21 metres of water and plunging down to over 50 metres. The walls are covered in sea whips, sponges, red gorgonian fans and the everpresent sea tulips, but the real feature of this site is the fish. Kingfish, large schools of jewfish, yellowtail, bullseyes, trevally and mackerel swirl around the area acting like magnets to large groups of grey nurse sharks, plus whaler sharks in lesser numbers.

Just about any pelagic species could pass by, and over the years, divers have reported sightings of hammerheads, marlin, makos and even tiger sharks. The Pinnacles is an excellent dive and usually produces more sharks than the gutters off Big Seal Rock. Unfortunately, the excessive depth limits bottom time, and is unsuitable for novice divers or photographers who like staying under forever. Expect a minimum depth of at least 36 metres depending on where you anchor.

There are many reef dives, all featuring a variety of sponge gardens, sea whips, soft corals, cuttlefish, moray eels, blue devils and lots of reef fish including wobbegongs and Port Jackson sharks. Divers can even find the occasional weedy seadragon. One site features fat blue wrasse which will take bait from your hand. Another site has a resident logger-head turtle which can also be handfed.

Seal Rocks is also known for its shipwrecks. The SS *Catterthun* was a 100-metre long inter-colonial trader, used to transport cargo and passengers between ports all along the eastern seacoast of Australia, travelling, ultimately, to Hong Kong. Her cargo frequently included gold sovereigns belonging to various banks and merchants along the route.

Battling a gale, the SS *Catterthun* struck a reef south of Little Seal Rock in the early hours of 8 August 1895, and sank 45 minutes later. Four passengers and 16 crew, all crammed in one lifeboat, survived the stormy night and were picked up the next morning by a fishing vessel. Fifty-five perished.

The SS *Catterthun* would have rested in peace had it not been for the 9000 gold sovereigns she was carrying, and a year later (in 1896), insurance companies ordered the recovery of this valuable cargo. At a depth of over 50 metres, this was a record-breaking recovery performed by two daring Australian divers using the traditional hard-hat diving equipment. In all, over 8000 gold sovereigns were recovered with some 800 left behind, supposedly because they had fallen out of the storage boxes. Speculation has always existed regarding these 800 coins. Some believe that the salvage team shared them amongst themselves, but others believe they're still down there just waiting to be found.

TOP: The blue groper is actually a species of wrasse.

CENTRE: Wobbegong sharks look docile but are snappy.

BOTTOM: Divers can get quite close to grey nurse sharks.

ABOVE: *Grey nurse sharks are found in gutters surrounding Big Seal Rock.*

OPPOSITE TOP: *The SS Catterthun sank with 9000 gold sovereigns on board.*

OPPOSITE BOTTOM: *The SS Satara rests in 42 metres.*

Resting on the sand in 60 metres of water, the SS *Catterthun* sits upright, but the sides have collapsed and there is a jumble of wreckage everywhere. The bow is reasonably intact and lying on one side. Winches, anchors and piles of anchor chain litter the area. On the side of the bow, the letters 'HUN' can still be seen—indisputable proof of the wreck's identity.

In the middle section, a large engine block looms up like a giant tombstone. The stern post is still in place, although the propeller is missing, perhaps broken off when the ship struck the reef.

The SS *Catterthun* is frequently visited by schools of fish and even the occasional sea lion. The necessarily long decompression stops present ample opportunities to see pelagic animals such as marlin and even small whales such as false killer whales and minke whales. Divers doing long decompression stops in summer are often visited by overly inquisitive dusky whaler sharks.

Another good shipwreck in the Seal Rocks area is the SS *Satara*. A 125-metre long cargo ship, the *Satara* struck a reef and sank in April 1910, only 15 years after the *Catterthun*. Scuba divers only discovered its location in 1984.

Resting in 42 metres of water, the *Satara* is fairly broken up and only the stern bears any resemblance to a ship. Hundreds of red morwong hang near the stern section and the massive four-bladed propeller dwarfs divers who move in for a closer look. The stern is the most popular section of the wreck and on days with strong surge, divers can be thrust quite forcefully through the blades—attesting to the efficiency of the propeller's design.

The engine and two boilers are still intact and the area is scattered with winches and flattened structural plates. The bow lies on its side with only the stem bar and a small section of the keel still visible. An old admiralty-style anchor lies on the sand, partially buried. Reef and pelagic fish swarm the wreck, and Port Jackson and wobbegong sharks can frequently be spotted resting on the wreckage. Whaler and grey nurse sharks occasionally cruise through.

Seal Rocks isn't always easy diving. Most sites are quite a distance from the town of Forster–Tuncurry, and in windy weather, it's a rough, wet trip to the best spots. But for those who persevere, or those who get lucky and have spectacular weather, Seal Rocks offers a diverse collection of amazing dive sites.

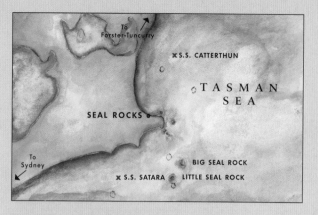

TRAVEL TIPS

GETTING THERE: Base yourself at either Forster-Tuncurry or at Seal Rocks. Dive operators will pick up at Seal Rocks beach with prior arrangements. It is a surf entry. You will need a car to get around.

BEST TIME TO GO: Seal Rocks can be dived year round. The clearest and calmest water is in autumn. The sharks are present all year round, but there is often a greater concentration in autumn and winter.

CLIMATE: 17–26°C between November–March, 8–19°C between April–September.

WATER TEMPERATURES: Summer through autumn (January–April) averages 20–25°C. Winter months average 15–20°C. The coldest month is usually September and the warmest month is usually February. Most divers wear two-piece 5mm wetsuits and remove the jackets in warmer months. A neoprene hood is useful in winter.

VISIBILITY: Can reach 40–50 metres but averages 8–20 metres. The clearest water is in autumn.

SNORKELLING: Snorkelling is available, but best organised as a separate activity to scuba diving.

OPERATORS

ACTION DIVERS (Tuncurry)
Tel: (02) 6555 4053, Fax: (02) 6555 3520
Email: diving@midcoast.com.au

BLUE WATER DIVERS (Forster) (also offers shark cage dives off the continental shelf)
Tel/Fax: (02) 6554 7478
Email: sharkdive@tpgi.com.au

FORSTER DIVE CENTRE (Forster)
Tel: (02) 6554 5255, Fax: (02) 6555 3622
Email: forsdive@atpgi.com.au

JERVIS BAY

ABOVE: Jervis Bay is a
protected wilderness with
few developed areas.

OPPOSITE: Old wives are
unique to Australia. The
dorsal spine is venomous.

Jervis Bay is a huge natural bay measuring 15 by 10 kilometres on the south coast of New South Wales, 200 kilometres south of Sydney and 150 kilometres east of Canberra, Australia's national capital. A protected natural wilderness both above and below the water, people flock to Jervis Bay throughout the year to unwind and get away from the pressures of nearby big cities.

The bay itself is lined with white sandy beaches which give way to towering cliffs on the north-east side near the heads. The surrounding bushland offers camping, hiking, mountain bike trails, bird watching and interesting tours of nearby ancient Aboriginal shell middens and rock paintings. One can even take a bush tucker tour, sampling natural savoury treats like berries, roots and witchetty grubs.

Jervis Bay is even more popular with water sports enthusiasts who sail, fish or simply potter around the bay...and who can blame them. From the main part of the bay, all you can see are natural shorelines. There's not a house or commercial development in sight, but not from lack of interest. Such a huge 'building opportunity' so close to two major cities doesn't go unnoticed, and over the years, various proposals have been put forward to develop a port, a commercial marina, a naval fleet base and armament depot, a steelworks and even a nuclear power plant. But Jervis Bay has many loyal champions and with an amazing amount of effort and determination, each new proposal was duly overthrown. Now the whole area, both above and below the water is protected by a network of national and marine parks, ensuring that Jervis Bay will remain a much-needed natural respite for a large portion of Australia's population.

The Jervis Bay Marine Park covers 22 000 hectares and includes the bay plus inshore areas north and south of the heads. Underwater, it is best known for the diversity and number of dive sites and marine life. It is also famous for offering a good spot to dive, regardless of the weather.

Inside the bay there are seagrass meadows, rocky reefs, caves, sheer drop-offs, tumbling boulders, kelp beds and even scallop beds. The nursery areas are home to seahorses, nudibranchs, starfish, blue-ringed octopus, sea hares, small cuttlefish and many species of juvenile fish. Nestled in the surrounding sandy areas are angelsharks and shovelnose rays.

Jervis Bay is fast becoming known internationally as a shark capital for film crews. Grey nurse sharks, wobbegongs, angelsharks, Port Jacksons and even saw sharks are reasonably predictable during certain times of the year, and international film crews are flocking to the area for one-stop shopping when producing shark documentaries.

The horn shark phenomenon in Jervis Bay is particularly interesting. During their mating season (late July through September) Port Jackson sharks, and in lesser numbers crested horn sharks, congregate en masse, often piling several deep in gutters, offering divers ample opportunities to get a close look at these relatively harmless sharks. Come October, the eggs begin to hatch and in some areas, the bottom is littered with baby horn sharks. Looking more like toys than live animals, one could be forgiven for thinking that a truck full of rubber toy sharks had overturned nearby and spilled into the bay.

A popular international celebrity in Jervis Bay is the weedy seadragon. Indigenous to Australia, weedies can be found throughout temperate Australian waters, but they're a sure thing in Jervis Bay. With a practised eye, divers can find seadragons virtually anywhere inside the bay, but one of the most popular dragon dives is The Docks on the northern side of the bay.

Numbers remain constant throughout the year and in late October, seadragon eggs, which are attached under the males' tails, begin to hatch. Eagle-eyed divers might encounter newly-hatched juveniles in December and January, no bigger than 2 or 3 centimetres. Usually these 'weedlets' hover in sandy pockets between rocks, protected from the surge. Look for swarms of tiny shrimp called mysids which resemble mosquitos. The juvenile dragons feed on these.

Yet another celebrity in Jervis Bay is the giant cuttlefish. Giant cuttlefish are the largest cuttlefish species in the world, reaching almost a metre in length, and can be found throughout temperate Australian waters. During their mating season (May to July), they are another sure thing in Jervis Bay and cuttlefish sightings are very common both inside the bay and along the coastline. The large males stand guard while smaller females lay their eggs, and when divers encounter a motionless male under a ledge or in a cave, chances are there's a female further back laying her eggs.

The females die after completing their first reproductive cycle. It isn't clear yet but males might survive several seasons before dying. Towards the end of the mating season, dead cuttlefish drifting on the surface are a common sight and many large cuttlebones (yes, the ones you put in your bird's cage) can be found washed up on beaches.

Unlike squid which lay their eggs just about anywhere, cuttlefish are more discerning and divers have to look in the back of caves and deep under ledges to find the distinctive ping-pong shaped clutches which begin hatching around October and carry on until early December.

A popular dive site inside the bay is a nearly-intact Fairy Firefly fighter plane which crashed after a mid-air collision during a training exercise in 1956. Its location was not well known to divers until the early 1980s, but is now visited frequently. Sitting upright in 16 metres of water, it is reasonably intact except for a missing section of one wing, but it has been heavily looted. Nevertheless, the infrastructure is still there and the Firefly is an interesting dive, often done at the end of the day when a shallow site is required. Located deep within the bay, visibility is frequently limited.

ABOVE: Giant cuttlefish can often grow to one metre in length.

OPPOSITE LEFT: A colony of fur seals moves in during the winter months.

OPPOSITE RIGHT: The Red Indian fish is a permanent resident at The Docks.

While the main attractions inside the bay are the animals, it's the terrain and often exceptionally clear water which entices divers outside of the bay. Edged by vertical cliffs which plunge equally vertically underwater, the coastline offers miles of excellent diving both north and south of the heads. There are caves, tunnels and massive underwater arches which are home to wobbegongs, horn sharks, rays, cuttlefish, sea tulips, nudibranchs, starfish and beautiful encrusting jewel anemones.

In some areas, the outside terrain is a series of terraces which step down to 40 metres and more. From 30 metres onwards, divers will encounter lush sponge gardens, plus fields of sea whips which are sometimes so thickly covered with white swimming anemones that it looks like it has been snowing underwater.

During winter and early spring (July to early December) when the water is at its coldest, a colony of fur seals move into a little alcove several kilometres south of the heads. Sleeping on the surrounding rocks, they enjoy almost perfect camouflage and many approaching boats have been initially disappointed, thinking the seals weren't 'home'. But as soon as the seals detect the boat, they leap from the rocks with resounding splashes and head out to greet their visitors. Females and juveniles are exceptionally playful and love nothing more than to frolic with divers, both on the surface and on the bottom. They zoom in and out amongst the divers, leaving a jet stream of bubbles behind them, created from air trapped in their fur. They nibble on snorkels and even blow bubbles in divers' faces. Occasionally the large males try to instil a more sombre note, but everyone (seals and divers alike) simply ignore them.

When Jervis Bay is good, it's very, very good. When it's bad, it can be shocking. In summer, afternoon winds howl and while there's always a protected spot offering an interesting dive, getting to and from that spot can be uncomfortable. The water is very cold during winter and doesn't warm up until after Christmas. But the animals and spectacular terrain make up for the hardships sometimes encountered, and when you hit one of those perfect days, when the visibility is 30+ metres and the water is dead calm, you'll think you've died and gone to heaven.

Cuttlefish, like their cousin the octopus, can change colours in an instance, with the most spectacular colour changes taking place when stalking prey, mating or when they feel threatened. Divers who have the patience to follow a large cuttlefish as it moves from sand to kelp to rocky reef will be treated to a fascinating array of colour changes as the threatened animal tries to blend into the various backgrounds.

ABOVE: Mating nudibranchs.

OPPOSITE TOP: Giant cuttlefish lay eggs deep inside caves.

OPPOSITE LEFT: Horn shark hatchling.

OPPOSITE CENTRE: Eastern blue devil.

OPPOSITE RIGHT: Saw shark.

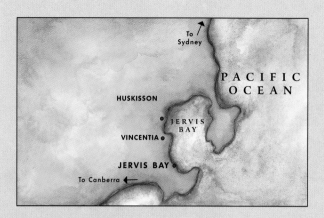

TRAVEL TIPS

GETTING THERE: The closest international airport is Sydney. Car hire is recommended.

BEST TIME TO GO: All year round.

CLIMATE: 16–24°C between November–March, 9–20°C between April–September.

WATER TEMPERATURES: 10–24°C. Water can be warm from summer to early winter (January–May), but cold winter waters persist until January.

VISIBILITY: Averages 20 metres but can exceed 30 metres in winter (June–September).

SNORKELLING: Some snorkelling but not at the dive sites. Snorkelling is best chartered separately.

OPERATORS

Liveaboards

JERVIS BAY CHARTERS, MV *Indulgence*

Tel: (02) 4441 7107, Mobile: 0411 514 235

Internet: www.jervisbay.com

OCEAN TREK DIVING RESORT

Tel: (02) 4441 6232, Mobile: 0413 759 649

Internet: www.oceantrek.com.au

Day Charters

PRO DIVE JERVIS BAY

Tel: (02) 4441 5255, Fax: (02) 4441 7113

Internet: www.prodivejervisbay.com.au

JERVIS BAY SEA SPORTS

Tel: (02) 4441 5012, Fax: (02) 4441 6723

Internet: www.shoal.net.au\~jbseasports

PADDY PALLIN ADVENTURE

Tel: (02) 4441 7448, Fax: (02) 4441 7465

Internet: www.jervisbayadventures.com.au

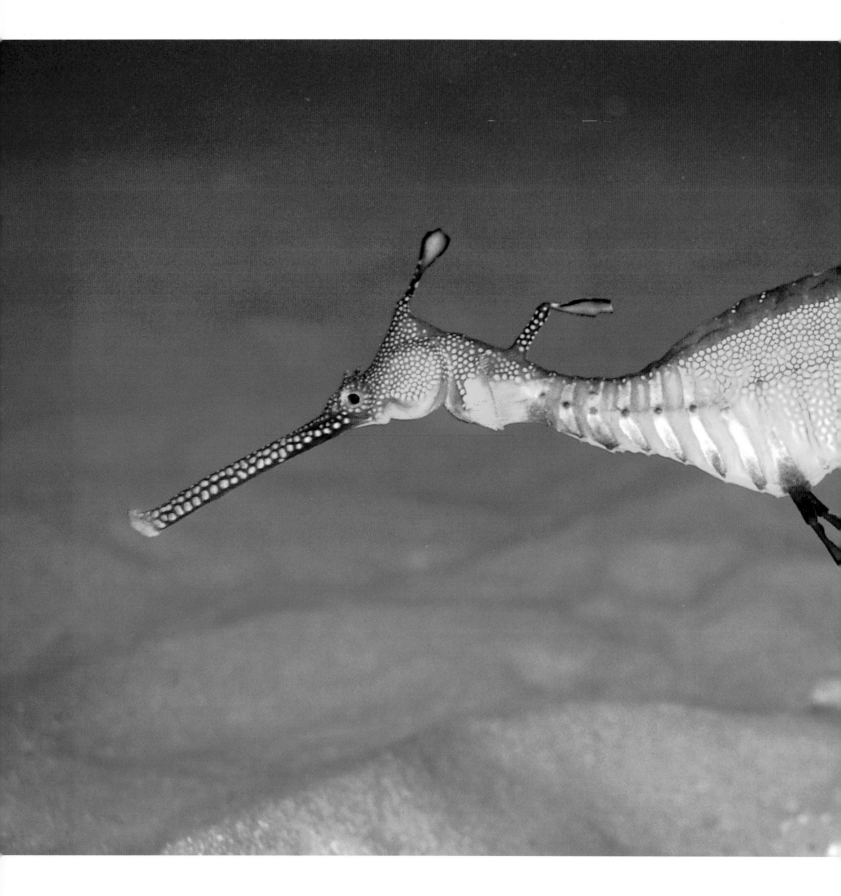

ABOVE: *Weedy seadragons are unique to Australian waters. Related to seahorses, the male incubates eggs under its tail.*

WILSONS PROMONTORY

ABOVE: Australian fur seals circle the boat, waiting for divers.

OPPOSITE: Perch hover near a tiny sea fan under a rock ledge.

Wilsons Promontory is a rugged peninsula located 200 kilometres south-east of Melbourne and is all that remains of an ancient land bridge which once connected Victoria to Tasmania. It is nearly 50 000 hectares in size and features cloud-topped mountain peaks, sweeping plains, plunging granite cliffs and picturesque bays. Its beauty has long been recognised and the entire area was declared a national park early last century. The surrounding 130 kilometres of coastline and nearby islands is a marine park which is multi-zoned to cater for a variety of marine activities.

The only settlement is a camp ground at Tidal River, located about 15 kilometres north of the southern tip on the west coast of the peninsula. This is an idyllic holiday retreat for campers, offering tent and caravan sites, plus a variety of cabins which can sleep from six to 30 people. The wildlife is rich, featuring friendly kangaroos and wombats, plus flocks of beautiful rosellas, offering non-stop entertainment. The adjacent river and beach provide hours of water fun and are safe for children. A small general store, café, and ranger's station/tourist information centre make roughing it easy and comfortable. There's even an open air cinema offering a rustic Australian experience which simply can't be missed. Wilsons Promontory, or simply the Prom as the locals prefer to call it, is a slice of Australian natural beauty at its best, both above and below the water.

Dive sites at the Prom range from shallow weed beds to deep wrecks, and cater to all levels of divers. The typical terrain is a boulder-stacked slope covered in kelp down to about 20 metres, and then sponge gardens and soft corals down to the sand at around 40 metres. The rounded boulders can often be as large as houses, and when stacked on top of each other, form a labyrinth of caves and swim-throughs. The slopes can be gentle or dramatic, and it is not uncommon to be in 60 metres of water only 20 metres from shore! Because of the quick drop off, most dive sites are very close to the shoreline of either the Prom itself or the surrounding islands.

Diving Wilsons Prom is by boat and the intended dive sites dictate the departure location for divers. If diving the west coast, the closest departure is at Tidal River on the Prom itself. Only small boats (around 5 metres) can be launched there, but the advantage is the close

proximity to the western islands and the southern tip of the peninsula (approximately 20 kilometres). If diving the east coast, most divers depart from ports north of the Prom. The trip from these ports can be 60 kilometres or more, and larger boats are required.

On the east coast, a favourite dive is the wreck of the *Lady Mildred*, a steamer which, so the story goes, sank in 1909 after sailing straight into cliffs just south of Waterloo Bay during heavy fog.

This dive site has a sloping, rocky bottom, covered with weed and kelp down to 18 metres. Beams and bits of wreckage are strewn about, and fossicking amongst the rocks can usually turn up small fittings or interesting trinkets. But remember, the *Lady Mildred*, like most wreck sites around Australia, is protected and nothing can be removed. A boiler and some machinery can be found near the sand at 24 metres.

Even without the wreck, this is a great dive site, as the rocky slope has many small caves and crevices which shelter perch, banded and magpie morwong, blue throat wrasse, Port Jackson sharks, hulas, and many other species of fish.

Further down from the *Lady Mildred*, just south of Refuge Cove, is Larkin's Cave. A small opening nestled in weed and rocks at 6 metres leads to a tight passage which eventually opens up to a large chamber. Leading off from the chamber are a few dead-end passages, but one allows further penetration to a completely enclosed rock pool located some 20 metres inside the rocky shoreline. The only way out is back the way you came, so watch your air carefully. Although this is a shallow dive, allowing a long bottom time, proper cave diving practices, including the use of cave diving reels, should be followed.

On the west coast, some of the more popular dive sites are adjacent to the offshore islands in the Anser and Glennie

groups. Skull Rock is the popular name for Cleft Island, located in the Anser Group, approximately 15 kilometres south-east of Tidal River. Rising 113 metres above sea level, it evokes excitement with its skull-like appearance and vertical sides which plunge sharply into dark, ominous water. Depths can exceed 60 metres, and currents of up to 2 knots are common.

A split on the north-eastern edge of Skull Rock is the starting point of a triangular-shaped swim-through at 16 metres. Almost closed at the surface, it is only about 3 metres wide at the bottom. Australian fur seals often accompany divers as they swim through to a large cathedral-shaped chamber. At the end, a large flat rock juts out, forming a balcony of sorts.

Sea fans, soft corals, sponges, and solitary hydroids decorate the walls of the cathedral, and clouds of barber perch often veil the entrance. Most divers stall here to enjoy the breath-taking scene, then drop over the balcony to the huge boulders on the slope below. At about 25 metres, the weed and kelp give way to sea whips and sponges. The perch persist, and colours intensify as you go deeper. Dark caves beckon, and banded morwong offer to guide divers into the recesses. There's never enough time to see everything on this dive.

Towards the northern tip, at about 9 metres, there is a large cave with a flat floor and ceiling completely carpeted in jewel anemones, sponges and yellow zoanthids. Wrasse and marblefish play with the air bubbles caught in the ceiling, and seals like to come here as well. This site is worth many dives and is always a 'must do', even for regular visitors.

Australian fur seals are the icons of Wilsons Prom, and the seal colonies on Kanowna Island, also in the Anser Group, are very popular. There are many hundreds of seals, and numbers are constantly increasing. The most enjoyable aspect of frolicking with these aquatic puppies is that they really enjoy the company of divers.

By law, you cannot approach closer than 50 metres from the colony's beach, but this restriction presents no problems. As soon as the seals see the anchor drop, dozens of cows and pups cascade into the water and beeline to the boat. Their impatience as you struggle to get kitted up is quite visible, and the games begin as soon as you roll back into the water.

TOP LEFT: Warty prowfish are hard to detect as they blend well into their surroundings.

TOP CENTRE: Delicate solitary hydroids hang from ledges on the Balcony at Skull Rock.

TOP RIGHT: A tasselled anglerfish is almost perfectly camouflaged against its background.

OPPOSITE: The crayfish seem to know they are in a marine reserve and have no fear of divers.

ABOVE: *Barber perch veil*
the entrance to Cathedral
Cave at Skull Rock.

The best way to enjoy seals is to simply settle in the weed at about 6 metres. This depth allows sufficient water for the seals to frolic and perform their best acrobatics, while at the same time allowing them the option of simply hanging by their back flippers from the surface, eyeing off the divers.

Once the usual games of mimicking bubbles and racing around with bits of weed are over, the seals like to get really close. Brightly coloured snorkels and fins are grabbed and tugged, so make sure that that nice orange Nikonos V camera has a strong lanyard on it!

The most intimate experience is when a seal takes a diver's hand in its mouth and tugs gently. Despite their sharp teeth, no damage is done, even on bare hands, but it requires a great deal of trust. The slightest hesitation can be sensed and panic by either seal or diver can result in serious injury. The term 'wild animals' is hard to apply once you've been affectionately mouthed by a seal.

The breeding season is November, and during this period new pups begin their swimming lessons. Visiting during this period is not recommended. The enormous bulls become excessively protective of their harems, and great white sharks are drawn in by their favourite food—seal pups.

Great Glennie Island, part of the Glennie Group, is about 10 kilometres south-west of Tidal River, and is home to dozens of excellent dive sites. The west coast of the island has steep slopes of large boulders plunging down to over 40 metres. Initially covered in kelp and weed, sponges take over at about 20 metres and, once again, become richer and even more vibrant with depth.

The rounded boulders form many interconnecting caves, creating a system devoid of light and so vast that the entire dive can be spent inside. The entrances of these caves are rich in sedentary life, and act as sanctuaries for many species of fish.

The passage between Danniveg and Citadel islands, both in the Glennie Group, is protected from most westerly swells by a wall of boulders, which nearly breaks the surface. This protected area provides a safe playground for divers. A bottom of white sand at 20 metres creates a brightness not seen on 'bottomless' dives and the visibility always seems better at this site.

Cruising around the boulders which line the island are large schools of fish, but the real attraction on this dive are the caves in only 5 metres of water. Large sea fans with basket stars sit among sponges and ascidians while colonies of solitary hydroids and sea ferns carpet the floors. Yellow zoanthids compete fiercely with sponges for space on the walls and ceilings. Bare rock is virtually non-existent. With such thick invertebrate growth, good buoyancy must be maintained at all times, not an easy feat considering that the cave floors can rise and fall over 3 metres! Fish are more prolific at this site than anywhere else at the Prom, which is regarded as a second dive only because it is shallow.

These few sites only scratch the surface of the top spots located around Wilsons Promontory. There are many seal colonies, shipwrecks, sponge gardens and even a great dive amongst building rubble beneath a lighthouse.

Wilsons Promontory receives plenty of rain and strong winds. Big seas can spring up quickly, making most sites undiveable, and reducing visibility for days. But, for a good portion of the year, the winds can be light, and water conditions are often ideal, with visibility up to 30 metres. At these times, the diving can be described as awesome.

TRAVEL TIPS

GETTING THERE: The closest international airport is Melbourne. Boats depart from Tidal River, Port Welshpool and Port Franklin.

BEST TIME TO GO: Wilsons Promontory can be dived all year round. June through September offer the most stable surface conditions.

CLIMATE: 11–29°C between November–March, 8–15°C between April–October. January and February are the warmest months. July and August are the coldest months.

WATER TEMPERATURES: 10–19°C. Water can be warm from summer to early winter (January–April) and divers often wear two-piece 5mm wetsuits, but cold winter waters persist until January. Experienced local divers wear drysuits from April to January.

VISIBILITY: Best in winter (June–September), averaging 18 metres. Summer averages 14 metres. Light winds for a few days can produce visibility over 20 metres and sometimes up to 30 metres.

SNORKELLING: The shallow sites all provide great snorkelling, but sharks can be a problem during seal pupping season.

AIR FILLS: There are no dive shops on the Prom itself and divers should bring enough tanks to do all dives. Second tanks can be arranged with boat operators.

OPERATORS

NRG DIVERS

Tel: (03) 9876 6626, Mobile: 0417 384 080

Email: nrgdivers@hotmail.com

M.V. *Inspiration* is 24 metres of luxury liveaboard for 11 divers. For details telephone: (03) 5686 2466

PORT PHILLIP HEADS AND SUBMARINES

ABOVE: Portsea Pier is one of Melbourne's most popular dive sites.

OPPOSITE: Underwater at Portsea Pier. This is a popular night dive.

Melbourne, the state capital of Victoria, is the second largest city in Australia, and is situated at the apex of a huge inlet over 700 square miles in size called Port Phillip Bay. The mouth of the bay, formed by Point Nepean on the eastern side and Point Lonsdale on the western side is only 1.9 nautical miles apart and the tidal race created by this narrow entrance is known as the Rip. Tides often reach speeds of 8 knots through the Rip and this fast moving, nutrient-laden water is the reason why the Port Phillip Heads area is so rich in fish and colourful temperate-water invertebrates.

Just inside the bay are colourful reefs and walls such as Popes Eye, Foggy Reef, Boarfish Reef and Spectacular Reef. Ranging in depth from less than 10 metres to over 30 metres, many of these reefs have such thick encrusting growth on the bottom and along the walls that managing neutral buoyancy is essential. Acres of bright yellow zoanthids compete for space with soft corals and sponges which range in colour from yellow, orange and red, to light blue and even a rich magenta. Small and delicate gorgonian fans on the walls also provide a kaleidoscope of colours. Dark brown, red, orange and yellow are the norm, but on occasion, divers encounter white, lilac and apricot-coloured fans, too.

Nestled in amongst this riot of colour are sea stars such as the biscuit star and ocellate starfish along with several species of nudibranchs including a very beautiful yellow species with white spots called a golden dorid. Look closely on sponges and curly bryozoans for tiny yellow sea spiders. Also hiding out on the reef are southern rock lobsters and hermit crabs.

Further colour swirls over the reef in the form of a variety of reef fish. Beautiful western blue devils peek out from under ledges, and brilliant green and yellow senator wrasse frequently hover over kelp beds. An exceptionally curious fish, senator wrasse always need to know what's going on and regularly swim up to divers to check them out. Beautiful silver and black boarfish cruise the area and colourful six-spined leatherjackets are abundant, too.

Sometime during your dive, have a quick glance out to the open water. Barber and butterfly perch regularly hover in slight currents off the walls and occasionally, large pelagics such as kingfish and pike swoop in to scrutinise divers.

This area is also popular for night dives. Filter feeders such as fans and soft corals extend their polyps at night, providing even more colour on the reef. Many of the fish are more approachable at night and quite a few change colours, such as the common goatfish which changes from silver and beige to a vivid red after dark.

At some stage through the night dive, try turning off your torch to witness the bioluminescence which is so famous in temperate waters. Any movement mid-water by a fish or your buddy's fins can be easily detected by a swirl of sparkling lights, and you can even decipher where ledges end by the blinking lights settling on the substrate.

The most popular shore dive inside the bay is Portsea Pier. Because it is shallow and close to amenities, this spot is popular with training agencies and many a Melbourne diver has learned to dive at Portsea Pier. Experienced divers return time and time again to hunt for weird and unusual macro life.

The pylons support a mix of kelp and encrusting sponges and hide small marine animals such as nudibranchs, marblefish, blennies and crabs. Mixing on the bottom either on the sand or in the rubble, divers regularly find seahorses, weedy seadragons, pipefish and goblinfish.

Portsea Pier is also an extremely popular night dive. It does not require slack water and the structure itself prevents divers from getting lost. This is the time you'll find dumpling squid, octopus, flounder and velvetfish.

Located just inside the Rip is one of the most popular dives in the area, Lonsdale Wall, which starts in 12 metres of water and steps down to over 60 metres in parts. Being so close to the Rip, the current usually screams along Lonsdale Wall and this spot is best appreciated during slack tide when a window of approximately 30 minutes of still water allows divers to take their time and check the area out carefully.

Descending the anchor line to a bed of lush kelp, take a second to get your bearings and then move across to the edge of the first ledge. At this point, the kelp stops and the colour begins. The first step is dotted with swim-throughs,

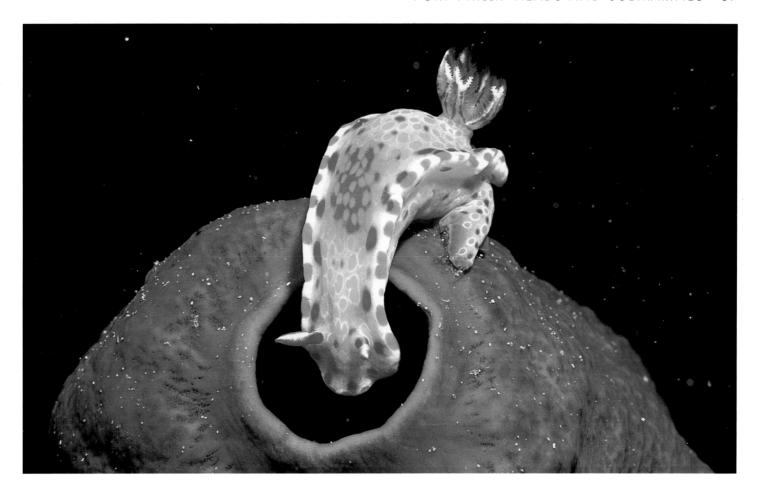

caves and ledges draped in colourful encrusting sponges, hydroids, ascidians and fans. Resting on one ledge, looking down to the next, it's difficult to resist going down just 'one more ledge', so be cautious and monitor your depth gauge and air carefully.

Experienced and intrepid divers frequently do drift dives in the Rip area. Small groups hold onto long lines with floats attached. Screaming along, this is no time to stop for a closer look. Instead, just enjoy the feeling of flying as you race over sponge gardens, bommies, ledges and drop-offs. Most drift divers surface after a pre-designated bottom time and usually the boat is right there to pick you up, having followed the float throughout the dive.

Drift dives anywhere along the Rip can be rewarding. The strong currents were responsible for the demise of many 19th century sailing ships which got caught in the current and couldn't manoeuvre clear of the rocks. As you drift along, look for the odd bit of wreckage, old bottles, crockery and ships' fittings. Prior to descending, take a landmark and then another when you surface. You will be amazed at how far you have travelled. Depending on the speed of the tide you can cover as much as 2 kilometres of underwater scenery without stopping, not that you could.

Outside the Heads, four J-class submarines lie scuttled in Bass Strait. After hostilities during World War 1, the British Admiralty presented six J-class submarines to the Australian Government as gifts. In May 1922, the decision was made to scrap the subs and they were

ABOVE: Nudibranchs are common throughout the Port Phillip area.

OPPOSITE TOP: A dumpling squid eats a shrimp under Portsea Pier.

OPPOSITE CENTRE: Six-spine leatherjackets have a venomous dorsal spine.

OPPOSITE BOTTOM: Flounders are flat and have both eyes on one side.

transported to the Flinders Naval Depot in Westernport Bay where they were stripped of all valuable fittings. Left to rust on nearby mud banks, the subs were finally scuttled over a four-year period between 1926 and 1930. Four were scuttled outside Port Phillip Heads. The other two were sunk as breakwaters on bayside beaches inside Port Phillip Bay.

Referred to by their 'J' number and depth, the J-1, like all of the others, has more than one name. Also known as 'the winged sub', 'the 36-metre sub', or 'the new deep intact sub', the J-1 was recognised by the veranda-like structure surrounding the conning tower. This structure was unique to the J-1 but in October and November, 1994, bad weather caused the collapse of the upright struts and upper conning thereby losing its 'veranda' appearance.

The J-1 can be penetrated via a hatch just aft of the conning tower. Only experienced divers with the appropriate qualifications and equipment should attempt penetration of any of the subs.

The J-2 also goes by the name of 'the broken sub', 'the deep broken sub' or 'the 39-metre sub'. It is thought that the J-2 must have hit the bottom at an angle when scuttled, causing it to snap in two. The break is aft of the conning tower, creating an easy entry and exit point to the hull. The conning tower of the J-2 is smothered in yellow zoanthids and surrounded by a number of perch and bullseyes.

The J-4 is 'the shallow sub', 'the 27-metre sub', 'the 90 footer', and 'the Bottom Scratchers' sub', so named for the dive club which found it. It tends to be the most dived submarine due to its comparatively shallow depth.

This sub is also broken forward of the conning tower which provides the easiest entry point for penetration. Inside the bow, which is accessible due to the close proximity of the break, divers can view the forward torpedo tubes.

The conning tower of the J-4 supports thick schools of butterfly and barber perch. Although numbers fluctuate, at times you can be 2 metres from the conning tower and not see the structure at all. The J-4 has the only conning tower shallow enough for kelp growth.

The J-5 is 'the intact sub', and as the name suggests, there are no breaks in the hull. As with the J-1 and J-2, it lies in relatively deep water outside Port Phillip Heads to the west. Its depth is similar to the J-1 at approximately 36 metres.

On this wreck, swim to the stern on the outside of the hull where you can see the prop guards and rudder. The conning tower is also home to perch and bullseyes and once again, covered with yellow zoanthids.

Whether you want to dive reefs, wrecks, jetties or submarines; look for fish, invertebrates, lobsters or seadragons; frolic with fur seals or watch dolphins riding bow wakes—you can do it all at Port Phillip Bay. The sites are easily accessible and serviced by dozens of dive shops. The water may not always be crystal clear or warm, but the diving is diverse and exciting. And after the dive, why not enjoy the many delights of Melbourne. Port Phillip Bay offers excellent diving in a very civilised location.

ABOVE LEFT: Pot-bellied seahorses can be found among kelp.

ABOVE RIGHT: Paper nautilus enters shallow areas to mate.

OPPOSITE LEFT: The conning tower of the J-2 submarine.

OPPOSITE RIGHT: The propeller shaft of the J-5 submarine.

TRAVEL TIPS

GETTING THERE: The closest airport is Melbourne.

BEST TIME TO GO: Port Phillip Bay can be dived all year round. The best time is late summer when the water temperatures are warmer and winds are favourable for getting outside the heads.

CLIMATE: Averages 11–29°C between October–March, 7–17°C between April–September.

WATER TEMPERATURES: 10–20°C. Water can be warm from summer to autumn (January to mid-March) and divers often wear two-piece 5mm wetsuits although most wear at least 7mm wetsuits. Cold winter waters can persist until November. Local divers wear drysuits from April to November.

VISIBILITY: Visibility tends to be tidal. It can range from 'not worth it', usually on outgoing tides, to over 20 metres. It averages about 9 metres.

SNORKELLING: Many good spots.

OPERATORS

There are many dive operators around Melbourne: For departures from Mornington Peninsula, try:

MELBOURNE DIVING SERVICES
Tel: (03) 9459 4111, Fax: (03) 9459 9942
Email: info@melbournediving.com.au
Internet: www.melbournediving.com.au

For departures from Bellarine Peninsula, try:

SOUTHERN CROSS DIVERS
Tel: (03) 5261 6466, Mobile: 0409 616 466
Email: scdivers@pipeline.com.au
Internet: www.pipeline.com.au/users/scdivers or www.divers.net.au

BICHENO

ABOVE: Governor Island is the centre point of a marine reserve.

OPPOSITE: Pycnogonids, or sea spiders, come in a variety of colours.

Bicheno is a tiny village located 185 kilometres north-east of Hobart on Tasmania's eastern coastline. Fishing is an important industry for the area and Bicheno has a small but active fishing fleet as well as a number of professional abalone divers. Located in an area known as the Holiday Coast, Bicheno is also a popular tourist destination. The climate is mild (by Tasmanian standards) and the kilometres of abandoned white-sand beaches attract many holiday-makers in need of a few days of relaxation. With a population of around 700, Bicheno offers a hassle free environment and tourists enjoy fishing, snorkelling, surfing, sailing, beachcombing and bushwalking. Divers from all over the world travel to Bicheno for world class, temperate-water diving.

Literally a stone's throw from the boat ramp is Governor Island, a narrow granite outcrop approximately 600 metres long and 150 metres wide. The island is an important sea-bird rookery and is home to one of Tasmania's largest breeding populations of crested terns. A semicircle of water starting approximately 400 metres north, arcing around 400 metres to the east and then 400 metres south makes up the Governor Island Marine Reserve, first proposed in the early 1980s and finally declared in 1991.

The entire Governor Island Marine Reserve is a 'no take' zone, meaning no fishing, netting or collecting (either live or dead material) can take place within the reserve. Only 3–5 minutes away by boat, this comparatively small area is home to some of Australia's finest cold temperate-water diving. There are dramatic granite pinnacles, gutters, vertical walls, caves, kelp beds, magnificent deep sponge gardens and mysterious kelp forests. Divers could spend weeks exploring the Bicheno area and still leave wanting more, not so much because there is a lot of area to cover, but because the marine life is so rich and densely packed.

Bicheno is best known for its deep-water sponge gardens, which are famous around the world for their thick, luscious growth and prolific fish life. Averaging around 30–35 metres in depth, the bottom is thick with a variety of sponges, including encrusting, tube and brilliant orange finger sponges which grow over a metre in height. Tangled amongst the sponges are ascidians, sea ferns, anemones, delicate sea fans, carpets of golden zoanthids and thousands of sea whips.

Living among these layers of immobile invertebrates are slightly more mobile animals, including starfish, flatworms, small snails and hermit crabs. Look closely on the tangled masses of bryozoans for tiny *pycnogonids* or sea spiders which are common in many areas of the reserve. Colourful nudibranchs can be found feeding on both the sponges and encrusting algae. Some species perfectly mimic their favourite food and are nearly impossible to detect, especially if the diver is influenced by mild cases of nitrogen narcosis.

The growth on the bottom is so thick that good buoyancy is a must. Often there are no places to land and the best you can do is find a spot for a single finger of support when taking a closer look. Watch your fins and make sure that, in an attempt to steady yourself, you aren't creating a cyclone behind you.

Swirling over the sponge gardens are clouds of fish, including mackerel, butterfly perch, pike, barber perch, bullseyes, wrasses and leatherjackets. Diving Bicheno's deep sponge gardens is truly a breathtaking experience. What a pity they are so deep. Divers could keep themselves entertained for hours down there.

Located in the same vicinity as the sponge gardens is a spectacular site called Golden Bommies. Consisting of two granite pinnacles which start in about 28 metres of water and plunge down to the sand at around 40 metres, they are absolutely smothered in sea whips, ascidians, bryozoan and sponges. The entire site is so thickly carpeted in yellow zoanthids that the whole area gives off a golden glow when viewed from a distance.

Tucked in amongst the encrusting growth are nudibranchs, shrimp, crabs, sea spiders, small cuttlefish and sea stars. Look on the sea whips and finger sponges for spidery basket-stars. Usually only unfurling at night to feed, at these depths they often unfold during the day, especially if it is overcast. Encrusting dead sea whips are beautiful jewel anemones, an invertebrate which Bicheno is particularly noted for. Ranging from a pale cream colour to a deep fuchsia pink, and sporting a fringe of delicate tentacles, it's easy to understand why these delicate animals are referred to as jewels.

The Golden Bommies are also a beacon to fish, attracting large schools of pike and butterfly perch, and offering refuge to reef fish such as boarfish, banded morwong and old wives.

Bicheno is also home to some interesting caves, ledges and swim-throughs, including The Castle. The first stop on this dive is a spectacular ledge near the base of some boulders at around 28 metres, and is often nearly obscured by schools of bullseyes and cardinalfish. Pushing through the fish, check out the walls, ceiling and rocky floor which are coated in yellow zoanthids and other invertebrates.

A few metres from the overhang, an enormous boulder rests against the main granite outcrop, creating a long, narrow swim-through. Check out the cracks and ledges along the walls of the tunnel for armies of bright red southern rock lobsters which are common through-out the reserve.

OPPOSITE TOP: With their swaying stalks and moody lighting, kelp forests can be spooky dives.

OPPOSITE BOTTOM: Bicheno is famous for its densely packed invertebrate growth.

On exiting the tunnel, swim up and traverse back along the open crevasse created by the top of the boulder and outcrop, checking out the colourful invertebrates and fringing kelp which grows on the sunlit reef tops.

On a calm day, the safety stop on this site is easy. Simply swim up to the top of one of the nearby pinnacles and explore the thick kelp. Sheltering underneath the thick blades are abalone, starfish, crabs, weedfish, octopus and small cuttlefish. You might even find a seahorse or two with tails tightly twisted around the stalks of the kelp.

With all this on offer, it's easy to understand why Bicheno is considered as one of Australia's top dive sites. But wait, there's more. Bicheno also has a few kelp forests, with the most popular spot located just south of the Governor Island Marine Reserve. True kelp forests are formed by a giant kelp called *Macrocystis pyrifera* which can grow to over 30 metres in length if given the right conditions and plenty of sunlight.

Giant kelp anchors itself to the rocky bottom with a tangled, root-like structure called a holdfast. Living amongst these root-like filaments are tiny snails, crabs, shrimp and nudibranchs. The surrounding rocky area is dotted with hundreds of abalone and patches of shorter kelp species. Cowfish, boarfish, and even the occasional weedy seadragon can be seen hovering in this area. A cousin to the seahorse, weedy seadragons are unique to Australian waters but are common throughout their range of southern temperate waters.

The spindly stalks of the giant kelp plant float towards the surface with the assistance of beautiful gas-filled floats found at the base of each blade or leaf. When a blade first appears it is small, as is the associated float, but as the leaf matures and enlarges, so does the float.

Giant kelp plants are virtually ecosystems within themselves supporting an array of marine invertebrates. Seahorses cling to the stalks and often swim from plant to plant; tiny snails in pastel-banded shells crawl over the blades, along with thousands of nearly transparent shrimp. Hovering mid-water in the kelp forest requires excellent buoyancy control, since there's nothing on which to steady yourself. But with a little practice, it's a technique easily mastered.

Divers who have never visited kelp forests often have a fear of getting hopelessly entangled, but this is unfounded. The kelp is not that dense and divers who move slowly and calmly can glide through the kelp effortlessly. If some part of your equipment does become ensnared, don't turn and twist—simply reach down smoothly and unhook the branch.

Diving Bicheno is well worth the effort. True, the best diving is in winter when the water is usually calm and clear, and true, serious cold-water protection is required. But just one dive and you'll be hooked.

ABOVE: Zoanithids cover the Golden Bommies.

OPPOSITE LEFT: Nudibranchs are found in the Bicheno area.

OPPOSITE RIGHT: This crab camouflages itself with a sponge hat.

OVERLEAF: The delicate polyp of a jewel anemone.

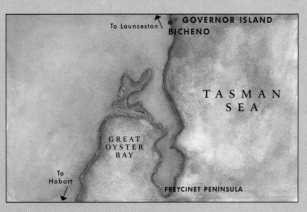

TRAVEL TIPS

GETTING THERE: Bicheno is about halfway between Hobart and Launceston. Fly to either town and hire a car. The drive takes around 2 hours. The Bicheno Dive Centre can provide transfers from Launceston airport with prior arrangement. There is also an overnight car ferry from Melbourne to Devonport. For more information, contact the T.T.-Line at Tel: 132 010 (within Australia) or (03) 6421 7333, or visit their website at www.tt-line.com.au.

BEST TIME TO GO: Diving can be enjoyed all year round, but the best conditions are generally between May and July when seas often become very calm and visibility is at its best.

CLIMATE: Averages 15–25°C from spring to autumn (October–April), and 6–16°C in winter (May–September). January and February are the warmest months; July and August are the coldest months.

WATER TEMPERATURES: Averages 11–14°C in autumn and winter (April–September). Spring and summer months average 16–18°C.

VISIBILITY: Visibility is best between March and July, averaging 20–30 metres and often exceeding 35+ metres. Spring and summer averages 12–15 metres, although the occasional summer day can put on 30+ metres visibility. During big storms, visibility can drop to 3–5 metres.

SNORKELLING: Excellent snorkelling from shore.

OPERATORS

There is only one dive centre in the area:
BICHENO DIVE CENTRE
Tel: (03) 6375 1138, Fax: (03) 6375 1504
Email: bichenodive@tassie.net.au

EAGLEHAWK

Seventy-five kilometres south-east of Hobart, Tasmania, lies the Tasman Peninsula, an area used from 1830 to 1877 as a penal colony for the very worst criminal offenders serving time in Australia's prisons. It was considered the perfect area for containing prisoners. The towering cliffs and surrounding cold seas prevented escape by water, and the only access to the main island of Tasmania was via a narrow land bridge known as Eaglehawk Neck. Only 20 metres wide at one point, it was easily guarded by soldiers and alert guard dogs, and few prisoners escaped the despair and hardship of this notorious penal colony.

Today, the Tasman Peninsula enjoys a much happier life as a tourist destination. Visitors come to enjoy the unspoiled natural landscape of rolling green hills and dramatic cliffside vistas. Rock climbers flock to the area to scale the peninsula's vertical pinnacles that speckle the coastline, and scuba divers travel to the east coast of the Tasman Peninsula to enjoy spectacular giant kelp forests, mysterious ocean caves, historical shipwrecks and a fascinating collection of temperate water marine animals. Diving is serviced by a single dive shop located at Eaglehawk Neck and divers generally refer to this destination simply as 'Eaglehawk'.

The giant kelp forests are always everyone's first stop. The closest thing yet to Jack's proverbial beanstalk, giant kelp grows at a phenomenal rate of up to half a metre a day in ideal conditions. Once it reaches the surface, it continues to grow, creating a swirling raft of gold and olive hues which twinkle in the sunlight.

Rolling back from the boat for the first dive can be disconcerting as most divers are sure that they'll get hopelessly entangled in the kelp. But this doesn't actually happen. While the kelp may look thick on the surface where it is rafting, underwater it looks more like groves of saplings. There's lots of space between the plants and divers can move smoothly through the kelp with a minimum of fuss. Should a gauge or fin strap get snagged on a leaf or stalk, simply reach down and unhook it. Wild thrashing and panicking serve no useful purpose and cutting it with a knife is both excessive and uses up valuable bottom time.

Slowly sinking to the bottom, you'll quickly be mesmerised by the muted illumination and flickering light rays which dance through the forest. The bottom is a rocky terrain with patches of shorter, bushier kelp. Clinging to the rocks are thousands of abalone and several

beautiful species of nudibranchs including a spectacular pink and orange long-tailed nudibranch which can reach almost 15 centimetres in length. Both yellow and banded sea spiders are common and usually found on curly bryozoa.

Weedy seadragons can often be found at the base of the giant kelp, hovering around the entangled root structure. They also frequently lurk near the sand-reef interface, at around 18–21 metres. Looking just like kelp, it takes a keen and practised eye to spot a weedy seadragon.

After checking out the bottom, it's time to begin a very slow ascent, examining the mid-water inhabitants. Kelp forests are like rainforests and feature nearly complete ecosystems throughout the various depths. Seahorses can be found hanging on to the stalks or even swimming between plants at virtually all depths. They can be well camouflaged, often assuming the same pale-brownish green colour as the giant kelp blades, and divers need to move slowly in order to spot these small animals. Hanging mid-water in the forest will be a real test of buoyancy since, unlike wall diving, there is nothing solid to hang on to.

Look closely at the kelp blades themselves and you'll discover that they are home to many small marine animals. Miniature starfish no bigger than your fingernail cling to the blades along with fascinating, nearly transparent shrimp. Extend your hand towards the tiny shrimp and watch them fearlessly leap onto you, perhaps assuming that you're carrying edible parasites.

The eastern coast of the Tasman Peninsula is riddled with caves both above and below and these make for exciting dives. Most impressive for its sheer size and grandeur is Cathedral Cave. With a maximum depth of 21 metres, this huge submerged cave has three large entrances. Running along the main chamber's walls is a suspended shelf about 1½ metres deep and about 4 metres from the ceiling. On this shelf, and on most of the walls, is a rich garden of sea life, including sponges, bryozoans, hydroids, golden zoanthids, a variety of jewel anemones, featherstars, shrimp and Eaglehawk's ever-present battalions of crayfish.

Dogleg Cave is another 'must do' dive at Eaglehawk. With a depth of 13 metres, its entry is partly obscured by tall sargassum weeds and bushy outcrops of the shorter *Macrocystis* kelp. The cave begins as a tunnel some 4 metres across and penetrates about 40 metres into the cliff before it turns sharply to the left and joins a larger, less adorned, tunnel. Divers can exit at the end of this tunnel or turn around and backtrack to the first entrance.

Within Dogleg Cave are deep ledges and small cul-de-sacs packed with a variety of invertebrate life all competing for a tiny space to call home. Much of the beautiful encrusting growth and invertebrates at Dogleg is similar to Cathedral Cave, but Dogleg also has the rare Ziebell's handfish (*Brachionicthys* sp). Well documented in this region, the Ziebell's handfish has yet to be described and therefore has no species name. It is related to the anglerfish and is a small, pale-coloured benthic fish covered in freckles. It has a small lure on its head and hops or walks, rather than swims, using modified fins which look a lot like legs.

South of Eaglehawk Neck lies the wreck of the SS *Nord*. On 8 November, 1915, the SS *Nord* was battling heavy seas. Deciding to take a calmer course, the captain cut between Big

and Little Hippolyte Rocks, not knowing that between them lay a submerged pinnacle, sitting like a dagger just beneath the surface, waiting to impale a ship. Interestingly, this same pinnacle sank the SS *Tasman* 22 years earlier, but the charts had never been amended. A valiant effort was made to save the ship, but the *Nord* took on too much water and was abandoned just north of Cape Pillar. Everyone escaped in the lifeboats.

Eighty-one metres long, the *Nord* rests in approximately 40 metres of water. Although the decking has collapsed, parts of the hull remain intact. The engine, boiler, propeller, propeller shaft and rudder are all still there. The bow is also intact but has broken away and fallen to one side. Nearby are several of the *Nord's* anchors. The hull is covered in a blanket of golden zoanthids, sponges, sea tulips, bryozoans

and sea whips. Masses of fish swirl around the wreck including wrasse, bullseyes and butterfly perch.

It takes several dives to see all of the *Nord*, but the effort is well worth it. Tucked into a little cove, the wreck enjoys a bit of shelter and it is an easy dive provided you are comfortable with these depths. Even the decompression stops are interesting and just about anything can happen. Depending on the time of year, divers are treated to a non-stop parade of amazing salps, thousands of jellyfish and bizarre comb jellies which pulse with fluorescent lights.

Another wreck off the Tasman Peninsula is the SS *Tasman*. Sixty-four metres long, the *Tasman* went down in 1883. This wreck was only located in 1998. Resting in 70 metres of water, it is rarely dived, and everything is still there, although somewhat jumbled due to exposure to

strong currents. There are port holes, bottles, crockery, an anchor chain and anchors. The boilers are still there, looming above the rubble and, although somewhat flattened, the basic layout of the ship is still quite discernable. The wreck is frequently swarmed by schools of fish and weedy sea-dragons can be seen drifting over tufts of kelp. Due to the excessive depths, access to the *Tasman* is restricted to divers qualified and experienced in the use of helium mixtures.

With all the fascinating kelp forests, caves and wrecks, it's hard to believe that there's still more. Eaglehawk also offers dramatic walls encrusted in thick growth and spectacular sponge gardens in deep water. Eaglehawk Neck is an exhilarating temperate dive, both in terms of visual spectacle as well as water temperatures which regularly dip down to a chilly 10°C in winter when visibility is at its best. Those who persevere, and those who invest in a good drysuit, are rewarded with adventurous diving experiences unlike anything offered on Australia's mainland.

ABOVE: The Ziebell's handfish walks using modified fins.

OPPOSITE: The SS Nord *is encrusted in yellow zoanthids.*

TRAVEL TIPS

GETTING THERE: Fly to Hobart. The Eaglehawk Dive Centre can provide transfers from Hobart airport with prior arrangement. Car hire is recommended. There is also an overnight car ferry from Melbourne to Devonport. For more information, contact the T.T.-Line at Tel: 132 010 (within Australia) or (03) 6421 7333, or visit their website at www.tt-line.com.au.

BEST TIME TO GO: The water is calmest and clearest from Easter until the end of August.

CLIMATE: Averages 10–19°C from spring to autumn (October–April), and 6–13°C in winter (May–September). January and February are the warmest months. July and August are the coldest months.

WATER TEMPERATURES: 10–13°C in autumn and winter (April–September). July and August are the coldest months. Spring and summer average 14–18°C. January and February are the warmest.

VISIBILITY: Visibility is best during winter averaging 20–25 metres, often exceeding 35+ metres during April through to August. Spring and summer average 10–12 metres but can sometimes drop down to 3–5 metres because of summer plankton blooms.

SNORKELLING: Eaglehawk is best appreciated on scuba but some dive sites offer interesting snorkelling including the kelp forests. The water is usually very cold, and even snorkellers require serious thermal protection except in January and February when a 3mm steamer may be sufficient.

OPERATORS

EAGLEHAWK DIVE CENTRE

Tel: (03) 6250 3566, Fax: (03) 6265 2251

Email: info@eaglehawkdive.com.au

Internet: www.eaglehawkdive.com.au

CAVE DIVING IN MOUNT GAMBIER

ABOVE: A well-equipped cave diver cruises through crystal clear water.

OPPOSITE: Sinkholes are smaller at the opening and wider on the bottom.

An important South Australian commercial centre, Mount Gambier lies 525 kilometres west of Melbourne, 450 kilometres south-east of Adelaide and only 25 kilometres north of the Southern Ocean. The city lies at the foot of an extinct volcano and there are four beautiful crater lakes in the region. Agriculture and forestry are Mount Gambier's major industries and the town is surrounded by groves of pine trees and vast fields of crops, cattle and sheep. Tourists flock to the Mount Gambier region for the beautiful scenery. Divers flock to the area to experience Australia's best cave diving.

Mount Gambier sits on a 100-metre thick slab of limestone which stretches from 50 kilometres inland all the way to the sea. Rainfall from further north seeps into the limestone creating an underground aquifer which flows slowly from north to south. Sometimes the water surfaces in small basins, creating ponds, and other times it scours through deep crevices, originally formed by geological upheavals thousands of years ago. In other places the water is so close to the surface that the land has collapsed, forming what's referred to as a sinkhole. Sinkholes tend to be deep and, in cross section, appear bell-shaped, narrower at the top, wider at the bottom and often with a cone of debris in the centre of the floor formed by the collapsing ceiling, and frequently augmented by the property owner's futile attempts to fill the holes.

All dive sites are on private or government-owned property, and due to a number of diving fatalities in the early 1970s, access is restricted. With only one exception, a Cave Divers Association of Australia (CDAA) qualification is required to gain access to the various sites. Visiting overseas divers should contact the CDAA to discuss their training and experience. In many cases, a temporary CDAA card can be issued.

The only site that does not require a CDAA certification is Ewen's Ponds. This is a set of three shallow ponds, filled with delicate reeds and plants, connected by narrow raceways. Crystal clear water, created by years of filtering through limestone, gurgles up from the sand in the first pond and begins its final journey to the sea. The water moves weakly through each pond, but the flow intensifies in the connecting raceways, making for exciting drift diving and snorkelling.

Access to Ewen's Pond is via a jetty which extends to the centre of the pond, thereby protecting the surrounding reeds. Entry couldn't be easier. Simply walk to the end, jump in and begin your drift. The centre of the pond is sparse with only a few plants scattered across a silty bottom. The visibility is nothing short of breathtaking.

The plant life increases as you drift towards the first raceway. Thick green algae appears first, followed by stiff reeds which reach metres out of the water. Long, soft fronds line the actual raceway, brushing against your face as you drift through. Tortoises, eels, fish and freshwater crayfish can often be seen, scurrying for cover as divers approach.

The second and third ponds are not as large as the first but the raceway between the two is longer, making for a very exciting drift. The third pond also has a jetty and this is where most divers exit. It is possible to continue drifting for another 2 kilometres to the ocean, but return transport would have to be arranged ahead of time.

Piccaninnie Ponds is one of Australia's best known and most popular cave diving sites, featuring a deep chasm and a submerged limestone cave called The Cathedral. First-time visitors are often disappointed upon jumping in because the visibility is never as clear in the pond as it is in the cave, but the anticipation is half the fun. Slowly moving through the water plants, never quite sure when

you're going to hit the chasm, your heart starts to pump and the adrenalin begins to flow.

Then, suddenly, you've arrived. At 16 metres, plant life disappears and the bare limestone walls begin to converge as they plunge into the abyss. Ocean divers never experience water clarity like this…you literally feel like you're flying. While it goes much deeper, divers are restricted, by law, to a depth of 36.5 metres. A plaque on the wall at that depth provides a sobering reminder that divers exceeding this depth in the past have died.

Fortunately, going deeper isn't necessary, since there's so much to see. One of the openings at the end of the chasm leads into The Cathedral. Sunlight streams through holes in the ceiling, dancing on the water's surface and illuminating the water-carved walls with a brilliant spray of light and shadow. There is life in The Cathedral, so don't be too startled if a short-finned eel or a black bream swims past the beam of your torch.

Engelbrecht's Cave, situated in a reserve in the main residential area of Mount Gambier, also provides a unique diving opportunity. Operated as a tourist cave by a local charity group, the tourists' adventure ends at the water's edge, just where the divers' adventure begins.

The entrance to Engelbrecht's West is like opening a lock. First you submerge and move forward half a body length into a tight passage. Then roll to the left, like a key in a lock, align your tanks with the shape of the slot and carry on until you reach a large white-walled passage. Only the first diver through gets clear visibility. The rest have to navigate by touch, until they clear the entry restriction.

Ninety metres long, the main passage terminates in an air chamber 40 metres in diameter and 13 metres high. Silence is normally associated with caves but this massive chamber is directly beneath the main highway and the noisy vibrations caused by large semi-trailers passing overhead can be disconcerting.

The Shaft is a fabulous, gigantic, water-filled cavern renowned throughout the international cave diving community for its unbelievable clarity and spectacular lighting effects, especially during summer when the sun, directly overhead, slices through the water like a bright blue, scintillating laser beam, spotlighting divers up to 60 metres below the surface like tiny blue dancers in a vast, darkened amphitheatre.

The Shaft was first discovered in 1938, when a plough horse stepped through the ground into a small, earth-filled entrance tube. The shape and extent of the cave remained a mystery for many years until the 1960s when divers made the first descent though an entry hole only 80 centimetres in diameter. There they were confronted with a 17-metre long underground lake.

OPPOSITE LEFT: The Shaft is entered via a flimsy cave diving ladder.

OPPOSITE CENTRE: An old petrol pump dumped in Little Blue Lake.

OPPOSITE RIGHT: A stark reminder that cave diving is serious business.

BELOW: Ewen's Pond can be dived by any certified diver.

Today divers share the area above the tiny entrance to the cave with some of the best Jersey cows in the country, as both gear and people are lowered into the hole via a tripod and caving ladder. Once floating on the water, divers don their gear and do a detailed buddy check before descending into a huge, darkened, bell-shaped subterranean void, 200 metres long and 97 metres deep.

Tank Cave is the latest discovery in the area and is proving to be unlike any other cave previously known in Australia. A tight restriction in a muddy puddle beneath a windmill frustrated divers for many years, but once this hazard had been successfully negotiated, determined divers were confronted with thousands of metres of passageway. Over 7000 metres have been mapped so far and Tank Cave appears to be a cross between a maze and an underground lake supported by massive columns.

Incredibly diverse, Tank Cave features large rooms, areas with different coloured silt, floors comprised of large clay blocks from bygone eras when the cave was dry, and complex sections of restrictive passages which lead from one section to the next. Tank Cave has great potential for expansion, and almost every new lead seems to open up into yet another large area with even more passageways which lead off to yet more uncharted territory.

Mount Gambier is the premier cave diving region of Australia and arrangements have been made with local land owners and government offices to allow access to over 30 cave sites. Each site is unique, both as a dive and as an experience. It's hard work and divers have to be highly qualified and very experienced to gain access to these exclusive dive sites. But for the fit and determined, it's difficult to beat Mount Gambier for sheer diving adventure.

ABOVE: The Chasm in Piccaninnie Ponds is nothing short of breathtaking.

OPPOSITE: The water clarity of Ewen's Pond has to be seen to be believed.

ADELAIDE

GULF
ST VINCENT

SOUTHERN
OCEAN

MOUNT GAMBIER

TRAVEL TIPS

GETTING THERE: Fly to Melbourne or Adelaide, and hire a car.

BEST TIME TO GO: February to May (late summer–autumn) has the most stable weather and pleasant air temperatures. December to February is the only time that the sun shines directly down into The Shaft. June to November are the coldest months; however, it is also the time when larger sinkholes are the clearest.

CLIMATE: February to May averages 16–24°C. November to February can be hot with air temperatures topping 40°C. June to August are the coldest months and air temperatures can dip down to 6°C.

WATER TEMPERATURES: The water is a fairly constant 14°C. In summer, most people wear a 7mm wetsuit or a drysuit. In winter, everyone uses drysuits.

VISIBILITY: Best in winter.

SNORKELLING: Great at Ewen's Ponds and no qualifications or permits are required. Also great at Piccaninnie Ponds, however a permit and booking are required. Contact: Dept. for Environment and Natural Resources on Tel: (08) 8735 1177, Email: tbarnett@deh.sa.gov.au, www.environment.sa.gov.au.

QUALIFICATIONS: Contact: CDAA at www.cavedivers.com.au.

OPERATORS

Air fills are available from:

Blue Lake Diving Supplies, Wandillo Road, Mount Gambier, South Australia, 5290.
Tel: (08) 8723 0879, Fax: (08) 8724 7776,
Email: info@bluelakediving.com
Internet: www.bluelakediving.com

The General Store, 50 Bay Road, Allendale East.
Tel: (08) 8738 7274.

RAPID BAY JETTY

Rapid Bay Jetty is a 500-metre long, T-shaped timber and steel jetty adjacent to the tiny community of Rapid Bay, approximately 90 kilometres south of Adelaide in South Australia. The original structure was built in 1865 to service local mining operations but this jetty was destroyed by storms in 1915. The existing structure was built in 1940 and used until 1990 as a limestone and dolomite loading terminal. These days, Rapid Bay Jetty is classified as a recreational jetty and is used primarily by fishermen and scuba divers.

The Rapid Bay community is small and puts little ecological pressure on the surrounding waters. Pollution is minimal, especially now that the limestone and dolomite loading has ceased, and visibility averages 7–10 metres. The depth is a constant 10 metres under the T-section. Surrounding the jetty are healthy grass beds and kelp outcrops, providing homes for many species including leafy seadragons, Rapid Bay's star attraction.

When it comes to wild and weird, it doesn't get much stranger than leafy seadragons, which are unique to Australia. Although related to seahorses, leafy seadragons can only be described as a piece of kelp which has broken free and become an animal, sporting leaf-like appendages, armour plating and short, spiky spines. There is little doubt that leafy sea-dragons would have played a large part in Greek and Roman mythology if only these ancient civilisations had known about them.

Leafy seadragons are found along the entire southern coastline of Australia, so they are not unique to Rapid Bay. But the population at this dive site is healthy and stable and the chances of sighting one (or two or three) at Rapid Bay are very good, provided you have a keen eye or you dive with a dragon-spotting veteran.

The big problem is their near perfect camouflage. Being poor swimmers, leafy seadragons survive by stealth, both to avoid predators and to sneak up on their prey. Their striped, leafy appendages and spiky armor blend in perfectly with the surrounding kelp, and their undulating, rocking-horse style of swimming mimics the to-and-fro swaying of kelp. Many a diver has 'lost' a dragon after looking away for only a split second. No, it hasn't dashed off; it has just blended back into the background, like one of those 3-D illusion posters where a hidden image appears and disappears, depending on how you look at it. The only way to relocate your lost dragon is to stop and look hard in the area where you last saw it. If you start

swimming around, you'll lose it for sure, and run the risk of kicking it with your fins.

Seadragons often hang in pairs so if you see one, stop immediately and look around before moving in for a closer look. Chances are there will be at least one more and sometimes several more in the same area. Being territorial, the same dragon, or pair of dragons, can often be found in the same general area week after week.

After you've had your fill of 'leafies' (usually about 30 or 40 dives), you may begin to notice the many other impressive features of Rapid Bay Jetty. The surrounding grass beds are rich with small fish such as cowfish, long-snouted boarfish, small cuttlefish and a variety of leatherjackets. Lurking under the kelp are large octopuses, and divers can often find the tiny blue-ringed octopus in old bottles or under the rocky rubble which speckles the area. Although not nearly as spectacular as the leafy seadragon, weedy seadragons can also be found in Rapid Bay.

Thousands of fish school under the jetty, including a very pretty silver and black species referred to as an old wives, which is also endemic to Australia. Usually old wives congregate in small groups of two to ten, but under Rapid Bay Jetty, they collect by the hundreds, drifting over the kelp and rubble. Golden bullseyes also collect in large numbers, drifting over the kelp and rubble but staying closer to the bottom than the old wives. Tiny baitfish collect by the thousands in the shadowy protection of the jetty, but marauding yellowtail are onto them and regularly zoom through, creating momentary silvery mayhem.

The pylons are a kaleidoscope of colourful soft corals, sponges, ascidians and starfish. Making their homes on the encrusting growth are blennies, gobies, nudibranchs and a variety of crabs including hermit crabs and decorator crabs. Hovering close to the pylons are juvenile and slow-moving fish such as globe fish, pygmy leatherjackets and tiny cuttlefish.

Beneath the jetty is silty sand sprinkled with rubble, discarded pylons and patches of kelp. Hiding amongst the rubble are frogfish, stargazers, tiny cowfish and lots of invertebrates such as crabs, shrimp and nudibranchs. Look carefully in little holes or under ledges formed by the rubble for decorator crabs sporting 'hats' of sponges or algae.

While the effort is well worth it, diving Rapid Bay Jetty is nevertheless a challenge. Some people enter from the beach and snorkel to the end, but the beach is rocky and if the wind and waves are up, a beach entry can be difficult. Also, it's quite a long swim from shore. Most divers prefer to enter and exit via a dive platform on the T-section of the jetty. Cars are not allowed on the jetty and it's up to divers to get their gear to the end utilising whatever their creativity can dream up. Prams, golf buggies, hand trolleys and skateboards all work equally well.

Once at the end, divers gear up on the jetty and walk down the stairs to a dive platform which stands 2 metres above the water (depending on the tide). From there, either do a giant stride entry or climb down a small metal ladder. A length of rope is handy for handing down cameras and hauling gear back onto the platform at the end of the dive.

Despite how special Rapid Bay is, its future has been unclear for several years. With its new classification as a recreation jetty, the responsibility for on-going maintenance falls under local government which was originally reluctant to take on such a costly ward, especially since some parts were in desperate need of repair.

At one point, proposals to remove the end section of the jetty, including the underwater pylons, were put forward, but the protected status of leafy seadragons and its recent declaration as the official South Australian Marine Emblem put pressure on local authorities. It has now been decided to renovate the jetty, including the installation of a new diving platform. Top marks to the local diving community and various environmental associations for this achievement.

ABOVE: Blue-lined octopuses are poisonous yet easy to overlook.

OPPOSITE LEFT: Cowfish hover near protective seagrasses.

OPPOSITE CENTRE: Camouflage crabs hide in sponges.

OPPOSITE RIGHT: Leatherjackets easily blend in with the pylons.

OVERLEAF: Slow-moving nudibranchs are popular with divers.

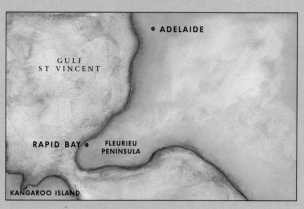

TRAVEL TIPS

GETTING THERE: Fly to Adelaide and hire a car. All diving is done from shore.

BEST TIME TO GO: Between October and May when winds are mainly from the east and the swell is minimal. Rapid Bay is influenced by south-westerly weather during winter (June–August), but the conditions are usually bearable. When the winds are westerly through to northerly, diving at Rapid Bay can be very uncomfortable.

CLIMATE: May through September experiences 7–17°C with the coldest months being June through August. October through April temperatures range from 10–27°C with the warmest months being January and February.

WATER TEMPERATURES: Summer months (November–April) averages 19–23°C. Winter months (May–October) averages 14–20°C, sometimes dipping down to 11°C at its coldest.

VISIBILITY: Averages 7–10 metres with extremes of 3–15 metres.

SNORKELLING: Excellent.

OPERATORS

The closest air fills are:

DOLPHIN DIVE

87 Main Street, Yankalilla

Tel: (08) 8558 2733 or (08) 8558 3950

Email: dolphindive@intertech.net.au

VICTOR MARINE AND WATER SPORTS CENTRE

160 Hindmarsh Road, Victor Harbor

Tel: (08) 8552 4757

WHITE SHARKS

ABOVE: The Australian sea
lion is prime food for
white sharks.

OPPOSITE: White sharks
willingly leave the water
to grab bait.

White shark! Just hearing these words sends shivers down most divers' spines, and invariably the *Jaws* music starts churning in the background. *National Geographic* underwater photographer, David Doubilet, calls white shark diving the 'big taxi ride'. You can sit on the boat for days with nothing happening and, as he says, 'the meter never stops running'. It's the most expensive trip a diver is ever likely to do and potentially the most disappointing. Shark sightings are few and far between and there are no guarantees.

Despite their high profile, little is known about white sharks (also known as great white sharks or white pointers). They are nearly impossible to keep in captivity and in the wild appear to be scarce compared to other widely-distributed sharks. Nevertheless, more attacks on humans have been attributed to white sharks than to any other marine animal. They are commonly found from southern Queensland to the North West Cape in Western Australia. The most frequent sightings are in Australia's colder southern waters.

The most reliable white shark diving in Australia is adjacent to a sleepy little town called Port Lincoln in South Australia, an area also known for its multi-million dollar southern bluefin tuna industry. Practising a form of aquaculture, the wild tuna are caught in nets and slowly towed back to holding pens where they are fattened up for several months before being slaughtered for the lucrative tuna markets in Japan.

Boarding a liveaboard boat in Port Lincoln, it's only a few hours to the Neptune Islands, south-east of Port Lincoln, just outside the mouth of the Spencer Gulf. Every operator has his favourite spot and if there are other operators in the area, they all try to space out. Once the anchor is set and the boat is settled, the berleying begins.

Many people resist white shark diving because they're afraid they will be revolted by a deck flooded with blood, guts and Australia's legendary legions of flies. But nothing could be further from the truth. Berley mixing is done in big vats mounted on the duckboard and an electric pump cleanly flushes the brew over the side in a continuous stream. There's little odour and it's unlikely you'll even notice that the berleying is going on.

Then the wait begins. The theory of berleying is to send a long, continuous slick of oil and blood out into the open ocean. Depending on the currents, slicks can be many miles long,

and the longer, the better. Should a white shark pass through a slick, it can determine the direction of its source, prompting the shark to, hopefully, travel up the slick to investigate and eventually arrive at the back of the boat.

Once a shark arrives, there's a mad rush to the cages. Different operators run things differently. Some have enough cage space for all their guests. Others don't and a roster system is devised. The cages themselves range from clear plexiglass tubes to mesh contraptions which look like refrigerators made out of aluminium door material. Floats are attached to the top of the cage and they float with the ceiling level with the water. You have to wear lots of weights to stay firmly planted on the floor of the cage.

Entering the aluminium cages also varies from operator to operator. The best option is to enter the cage while it is firmly on deck and then, using a crane, have the cage lifted, divers and all, over the side and into the water. Other operators have cranes which hold the cages level with the duckboard on the back of the boat. Divers simply step into the cage through a side door, close it behind them and get lowered into the water.

The most heart thumping option is to have to jump into the cage while it floats in the water, through a trap door on the top. This procedure is a little daunting the first time around. The crew drag the cages alongside the duckboard and as it wobbles around in the chop, you walk onto the top of the cage and jump in through the small trap door. This is terrifying stuff, especially when there's a big whitey swimming around underneath. The concept of missing the trap door and falling into the ocean, probably landing right on the shark, seems like a very real possibility. But you don't, and it's really quite an easy exercise.

Whatever the method, finally, you're underwater, face-to-face with White Death! First-time white shark divers are always amazed at how peaceful the sharks are. Television documentaries lead us to believe that white sharks are constantly thrashing and ravaging, but this only happens when they are teased with solid bait. Blood and oil attract

sharks, but their demeanour is that of curiosity. If there isn't any solid bait, they just mill around, living in hope. Most operators put out very little bait, since once a shark has had a few feeds, it tends to move off, making for unhappy guests. Sometimes the operators will hang smaller fish off the cages to encourage the sharks to move in close, giving guests a better view.

Underwater, it's quite surreal. Here you are, in a cage, which suddenly starts looking very flimsy, with a huge, dangerous shark only metres away. The cage is bouncing around in the chop and divers are being thrown about because they're too afraid to put their fingers through the mess to hold on. Every cell in your body screams fear, but for some inexplicable reason, you're not afraid. It's actually quite peaceful—probably the way you feel right before you die. The sharks just cruise around while you have the adrenalin rush of a lifetime.

After a few minutes things begin to settle down and you start becoming aware of your surroundings. You can see across the way to other cages, and even begin to notice individual markings on the sharks, if you're lucky enough to have more than one shark. Most cages have big windows to allow uninterrupted viewing, and photographs. As the sharks cruise by, you can even stick your hand out and touch them.

Sometimes the sharks stay for hours, sometimes they stay for only a few minutes. Sometimes you get a shark right away, sometimes it takes days, if at all, for a shark to arrive. Between dives, there's not much to do. Dinghies can transfer passengers to the islands which are worth a visit. They are littered with seal pups, offering great photo opportunities.

OPPOSITE: The first encounter is always scary and few divers venture close to the windows.

BELOW: After a few encounters, divers are keen to get as close as possible to the sharks.

ABOVE: Seeing a white shark underwater from the safety of a cage is one of diving's biggest buzzes.

OPPOSITE TOP: Entering the safety cages from the duckboard is an easy manoeuvre.

OPPOSITE BOTTOM: Laying the berley slick is a tidy and sanitised procedure.

Stay well clear of the big bulls, though, which can become aggressive if they feel their dominance is being threatened.

Some operators offer diving 'around the corner' while waiting for the sharks to arrive. These are often dives with seals, which can be fun, but the concept of swimming close to an area being berleyed for white sharks needs careful consideration.

Still other operators entertain their guests by doing cage dives on the bottom. Everybody jumps in and the cages are lowered to the sea bed. The water is usually much clearer under the berley slick and often well populated by rays, eel and crayfish, which are attracted by the minced bait that drifts down from the surface. Doing some preliminary cage dives is a good idea because you can get accustomed to getting in and out of the cages without the added concern of having sharks in the immediate vicinity. There's also always the chance that a shark will arrive while you're on the bottom. Seeing a huge white shark emerge from the edge of visibility, skimming across the bottom towards you is very exciting indeed.

But despite all the other entertainment offered to keep guests occupied, most people prefer to stay close by in case a shark shows up. They sleep, watch videos, tinker with their cameras or read. Bring lots of books!

Strictly for the deadly serious or the deadly rich, white shark trips are very expensive and there are no guarantees. Many trips see no sharks at all, so be prepared for the worst...there's always next year. But on the other hand, you could get lucky. There's nothing quite like seeing a white shark up close and toothy. Nothing will prepare you for its size, its amazing girth, or how majestic it is. It's the ultimate diver's buzz. Big risks...big rewards. That's white shark diving.

EYRE PENINSULA

To Adelaide

PORT LINCOLN

SPENCER GULF

NEPTUNE ISLANDS

TRAVEL TIPS

GETTING THERE: Fly to Port Lincoln from Adelaide.

BEST TIME TO GO: Trips traditionally operated during the seal pupping season which is late January through April, but in the last few years, many operators have discovered better action from late April to September with July and August being good months.

CLIMATE: January to April is usually fine with the occasional storm or strong wind. Air temperatures range from 16–24°C. Winter months (May–October), are colder, averaging 14–16°C. August is the coldest month with 10–12°C not unheard of.

WATER TEMPERATURES: 14–18°C in summer. Warm full-length 7mm wetsuits with hoods are recommended. Some people wear dry suits but they are not usually necessary in the summer. Temperatures drop to about 10–12°C in August (winter). Thick neoprene wetsuits are a minimum; drysuits are strongly recommended.

VISIBILITY: Five to 18 metres.

SNORKELLING: Not recommended.

OPERATORS

CALYPSO STAR CHARTERS

Captain Rolf Czabayski

Tel: (08) 8364 4428, Fax: (08) 8332 6360

Email: calypsostar@nbw.com.au

Internet: http://nbw.com.au/calypsostar

MIKE BALL DIVE EXPEDITIONS

Tel: (07) 4031 5484, Fax: (07) 4031 5470

Email: mbde@mikeball.com

Internet: www.mikeball.com

RODNEY AND ANDREW FOX

Tel: (08) 8376 3373, Fax: (08) 8376 3362

Email: rodneyfox@chariot.net.au

Internet: www.rodneyfox.com.au

THE WRECK OF
THE HMAS *SWAN*

ABOVE: The Swan was decommissioned by the Navy and donated to Western Australia.

OPPOSITE: In only 7.5 metres of water, the crow's nest makes an interesting safety stop.

Destroyer escort HMAS *Swan* was launched in 1967 and commissioned by the Australian Navy on 20 January 1967. It was 112 metres long, 23 metres high, 12.5 metres wide, and displaced 2700 tonnes. At the time, it was the most expensive warship ever built by Australia, costing $22 million.

For 26 years, HMAS *Swan* served Australia, travelling to both Australian and south-east Asian ports. It operated as a troop carrier escort during the Vietnam War and steamed approximately 800 000 nautical miles during its service life.

On 13 September 1996, the *Swan* was decommissioned and something unusual happened. Normally, decommissioned Australian naval ships are either sold as going concerns to 'friendly' nations or stripped and sold as scrap metal. But the *Swan's* fate was to be different. It was donated to the government of Western Australia who, in turn, invited expressions of interest from various community groups around the state.

There was no shortage of suggestions for the *Swan's* new life, including a floating museum, restaurant, church, and of course, a dive wreck/artificial reef. After careful consideration, the *Swan* was given to the Busselton Shire who handed the ship over to the Geographe Bay Artificial Reef Society to relocate and deploy as an artificial reef and wreck dive.

It took 12 months and over 10 000 people-hours for the Geographe Bay Artificial Reef Society and a slew of volunteers, many of whom weren't even divers, to prepare the wreck for safe diving. Miles of cables and nearly 7000 litres of fluids were removed. Because they can be hazardous to divers, the engine room and boiler room were sealed off. Access holes were cut throughout the ship with the goal being that divers could explore significant portions of the ship without ever venturing beyond direct line of sight of an entry or exit point.

Funding was a constant headache. As the ship itself was a gift, Commonwealth funding ceased at that point. But local government and businesses were extremely generous and raffles became a way of life in this small Western Australian community. But still it wasn't enough, and further scrapping had to take place. In all, over $90,000 had to be raised.

Choosing the site was also an issue. It had to be on a sandy bottom with no naturally occurring reefs or significant seagrass beds. It needed to be close to land, easily accessible via

local boat ramps and in an area which could be dived safely in most weather conditions. This protection not only offered comfort to divers, but would hopefully extend the life of the wreck. The depth had to be at least 30 metres if the ship was to stand upright and still provide government-required shipping clearances, but no-one wanted it to be any deeper. Currents couldn't be too strong and it had to be easy enough for even novices to feel comfortable. The perfect spot was found in Geographe Bay, 1.3 nautical miles off Meelup Beach near Dunsborough, a small community 300 kilometres south of Perth.

The scuttling date of 14 December 1997 dawned clear and the *Swan* was towed to the site and aligned with the bow pointing north-west into what would be the winter swell. At 11am, with more than 10 000 people lining the shore and over 600 spectator crafts, the charges were set off and the *Swan* sank in 2 minutes and 53 seconds, landing upright on the bottom. Within hours of her sinking, the

Swan was visited by fast pelagic fish such as tuna and Samson fish. Within days, slower moving fish had moved in, including an amazing school of globe pufferfish, a phenomenon confounding many scientists who did not believe this species schooled in such a manner. Within months, invertebrate growth was settling on the wreck and within a year, it was almost completely covered with a thin layer of encrusting growth and seaweed.

Diving the *Swan* couldn't be easier. Board a boat from either a boat ramp or on the beach and within 15 minutes you've arrived at the site. Being sheltered by the headlands, it's usually fairly calm, good news for divers with less-than-cast-iron stomachs. Once you're kitted up, simply jump into the water and follow the mooring line down to the wreck. Sometimes there might be a slight current, but there's always a leeside sheltered from the current.

Encrusting the decks is a thick growth which sways in the surge. Look carefully as it flops back and forth for huge bottom dwelling flatheads. Off the bow are the ever-present schooling globe fish. Along the port side which is more shaded, encrusting corals are growing beautifully. Look for gobies and nudibranchs in this area. Swimming along the hull, there are many access openings and divers can explore a number of rooms such as toilets, the galley and the bridge, as well as artillery magazines. Schools of bullseye have taken up residence in many of the rooms. Under the rudder is an eerie area that almost always produces some large fish, hiding out in the shadows. On your ascent make sure to check out the encrusting growth on the mast.

Keep an eye out towards the open water for King George whiting and bream which frequently cruise along the hull, and when making your final ascent look for the friendly batfish which often follow divers back to the boat.

Being the only 'reef' for miles, the *Swan* is a congregating point for ocean fish, providing a spot where they can both rest and hunt. To encourage the fish, and at the persistence of the Geographe Bay Artificial Reef Society, the Western Australia government has declared an exclusion

zone radiating 200 metres out from the wreck on all sides. Both fishing and hunting are prohibited. There is also restricted access to the wreck. Private boats need a licence, which is inexpensive to purchase and the fee goes towards maintaining the site and the moorings surrounding it. No more than ten vessels can visit the wreck at one time.

The popularity of the *Swan* took everyone by surprise. Overnight, dive shops were deluged with divers and within a year, many shops had been forced to upgrade or add to their fleets. During the peak season, some shops are running a double dive in the morning and then another double dive in the afternoon. Tourism boomed overnight, and associated industries such as restaurants and hotels also benefited. Local divers return every week to see what's new on this constantly changing and improving dive site. The *Swan* is also attracting intra- and interstate holiday-makers, as well as many overseas visitors.

The *Swan* is a prime example of what can be achieved when local communities and businesses work with divers, tapping into their unbounding enthusiasm.

ABOVE: The bridge is completely open and frequently filled with fish.

OPPOSITE: A diver swims along an external passageway.

TRAVEL TIPS

GETTING THERE: Fly to Perth, hire a car and drive to Dunsborough.

BEST TIME TO GO: November and May. The remaining months bring strong west and north-west winds which makes diving weather-dependent.

CLIMATE: A Mediterranean climate with hot, dry summers and mild, wet winters. Maximum of 30°C in summer and a minimum of 10°C in winter.

WATER TEMPERATURES: Summer months (November–April) average 19–23°C. Winter months (May–October) average 14–20°C.

VISIBILITY: Summer months can offer visibility up to 25 or 30 metres. Visibility can drop during winter.

SPECIAL NOTES: A small fee is payable for permits for private boats. Permits can be purchased from:

Dunsborough Tourist Bureau, Naturaliste Terrace, Dunsborough. Tel: (08) 9755 3299

Busselton Tourist Bureau, Southern Drive, Busselton, WA 6280. Tel: (08) 9752 1288.

OPERATORS

CAPE DIVE

Tel: (08) 9756 8778, Fax: (08) 9756 8669

Email: capedive@netserv.net.au

Internet: www.netserv.net.au/capedive

DIVE SHED

Tel/Fax: (08) 9754 1615

Email: diveshed@compwest.net.au

DIVING VENTURES

Tel: (08) 9756 8846, Fax: (08) 9756 8806

Email: diving@dventures.com.au

Internet: www.dventures.com.au

BUSSELTON JETTY

ABOVE: Busselton Jetty is one of the longest wooden jetties in the Southern Hemisphere.

OPPOSITE: Bathed in fresh ocean currents, the pylons are dripping with a variety of invertebrates.

Busselton Jetty is a 2-kilometre long wooden jetty situated adjacent to the booming little tourist town of Busselton, approximately 275 kilometres south of Perth in Western Australia. The original structure, built in 1865, was used for loading and unloading ships which in the first instance were predominantly whaling ships. Quite short in the beginning, Busselton Jetty was extended many times over the years to accommodate larger and larger ships.

As trade turned from whaling to timber, transferring cargo along its length became a problem, and in 1911, a tram was installed on the jetty, originally pulled by horses and later by small steam locomotives. Its use as a commercial dock ceased in 1972 and now Busselton Jetty is a popular tourist attraction, offering substantial walks for the hardy and pleasant train rides for the less than hardy. Unknown to most of its visitors, it's also a fantastic dive site.

The best diving is found in the last 100 metres which is regularly bathed by clean, gentle currents. Virtually every pylon is dripping with every form of temperate-tropical invertebrate marine life found in south-west Australia. In a classic marine battle for space, sponges, ascidians and corals fight it out under Busselton Jetty, leaving each pylon thick with several layers of encrusting growth.

Swarming under the jetty are large schools of pike and yellowtail which look like liquid mercury, streaming in and out of the shadows, as they weave through the pylons. Occasionally, large Samson fish or Western Australian jewfish will streak through, creating momentary mayhem. But as quickly as they appear, everything is once again peaceful and the fish resume their rhythmic schooling patterns.

The marine animals found under Busselton Jetty are like layers of an onion. Peel off the layer of pelagic fish and you'll find 'less pelagic' fish which are usually poor swimmers hovering close to pylons for protection. Very common in this 'layer' are porcupine fish. Even more plentiful but harder to spot are blennies which blend exceptionally well with their environment. Sometimes they simply cling to the growth on the pylons, but more frequently they find homes in dead barnacles, where they spend most of their time peeking out at the world. If you get too close, they quickly retreat, but usually their curiosity gets the better of them and before long, they're out again, challenging you once more to come too close.

Peel back the less-pelagic layer and you'll find benthic slow-moving creatures clinging to the pylons such as small crabs, shrimps and nudibranchs. Busselton Jetty is a nudibranch-lovers' heaven. Many species make the jetty their home, but the most common is a large, pink and orange one that grows to almost 15 centimetres. This beautiful nudibranch is so prolific that it sometimes 'rains' pink and orange nudibranchs, dislodged from the pylons by divers' bubbles. Less flashy, but possibly more fascinating are the nudibranchs which mimic their environment. One looks just like the polyps of the telesto coral and another looks just like the ragged encrusting sponge which it lives and feeds on.

The sea bed under the jetty is composed of sand and silt, littered with chunks of timber and bits of old pylons which have fallen over. Hiding amongst the fallen timbers are cowries, even more nudibranchs and several unusual species of fish, such as pineapplefish and frogfish.

Frogfish are particularly fascinating. Sporting appendages which look more like legs than fins, frogfish crawl rather than swim and attract prey by dangling a stringy filament in front of their mouth, hence their other name, anglerfish. Sitting motionless, they simply wait, and when a curious fish ventures too close, the frogfish gulp it down. Frogfish are more active at night, preferring to hide deep within crevices and under logs during the day. They look like globs of purple and pink encrusting sponges.

Cruising under the jetty, many divers encounter bird eggs lying on the bottom. No, they're not left over from a tourist's or fisherman's lunch. Pigeons nest in the rafters and their eggs regularly fall into the water. The fish love to pick out the insides, frequently leaving the shells virtually intact.

The entire jetty is surrounded by a further marine layer of seagrass which acts as an important nursery for juvenile marine animals. In recognition of their importance to the overall marine environment, many species of seagrasses are protected, and visiting boaters are asked to drop their anchors in bare sandy patches to avoid disturbing these delicate ecosystems.

Littered throughout the grassbeds are old discarded pylons and rocks which often look suspiciously like ballast blocks used in colonial trading ships. It's hard to believe that they would still be there after all these years, but one never knows. Hiding in the grass are octopuses, leatherjackets, other juvenile fish, and even more exciting... weedy seadragons!

Unique to Australia, weedy seadragons look like 30 centimetres long, stretched-out seahorses covered in blue and yellow spots. The Busselton seadragons are slightly paler than the weedy seadragons in New South Wales, but they are still beautiful. They're hard to spot because their camouflage is so good, but look closely along the line between the grass and sand, or right on top of the grass. To be fair, Busselton isn't known as a sure-dragon dive. Many local divers have paid hundreds of visits to Busselton Jetty and have never seen a dragon—their camouflage is that good! If you want to see one, ask a guide to find one for you.

OPPOSITE LEFT: This nudibranch reaches 15 centimetres in length.

OPPOSITE CENTRE: Fearless blennies live in empty barnacles.

OPPOSITE RIGHT: Starfish thrive under Busselton Jetty.

OVERLEAF: Colourful invertebrate growth under Busselton Jetty.

Diving Busselton Jetty can take several forms. The truly hardy do it from the beach, snorkelling under the jetty the entire 2 kilometres to the end. Others take the tourist train. For a small additional fee, scuba divers and snorkellers are welcome to load their gear onto the little train and ride it to the end of the jetty where there are stairs and a platform at water level. After the dive, either catch the train back; or do a one-way dive back to shore, switching to snorkel when your air runs low. The easiest way to dive Busselton Jetty is from a commercial charter boat. The boat ramp is adjacent to the jetty and the trip takes two or three minutes.

Diving a jetty for the first time can be a little unsettling. Going from the bright shallow waters surrounding the jetty to the dark gloom underneath takes a little getting used to. The pylons loom overhead and divers need to be aware of their fins at all times to avoid kicking the encrusting growth. But the rewards are great. The maximum depth throughout the far end of the jetty is a constant 8 metres, depending on the tides, and experienced divers can make a tank last for over two hours. Inexperienced divers can easily break the elusive '60 minute' barrier. Perfect for inexperienced divers, yet fascinating enough to entertain the most experienced veteran, Busselton Jetty is equally fascinating for snorkellers. It's also a terrific night dive!

On a final note, in 1999, Busselton Jetty caught on fire which resulted in the loss of a 20-metre section about 100 metres from the end. While a portion of the good diving has been destroyed, there is still plenty to see.

TRAVEL TIPS

GETTING THERE: Fly to Perth, hire a car and drive to Busselton. You will need a car to make your way to the boat ramp or dive shop.

BEST TIME TO GO: The best time to visit Busselton Jetty is between November and May.

CLIMATE: Hot, dry summers and mild, wet winters. Maximum temperatures reach 30°C in summer and a minimum of 10°C in winter.

WATER TEMPERATURES: November–April averages 19–23°C. May–October averages 14–20°C.

VISIBILITY: 10–25 metres is not uncommon during summer, depending on winds. During winter months, visibility can drop to around 3 to 4 metres.

SNORKELLING: Excellent.

SPECIAL NOTES

Busselton Jetty Train Service

Operates every day on an hourly basis between 10.00am and 4.00pm, no bookings required. All welcome. A surcharge applies for dive gear.

OPERATORS

CAPE DIVE

Tel: (08) 9756 8778, Fax: (08) 9756 8669

Email: capedive@netserv.net.au

Internet: www.netserv.net.au/capedive

DIVE SHED

Tel/Fax: (08) 9754 1615

Email: diveshed@compwest.net.au

CRAY Z CAT CHARTERS

Tel: (08) 9247 5243, Fax: (08) 9247 5875,

Mobile: 0417 928 100

Email: crayzcat@iprimus.com.au

ROTTNEST ISLAND

ABOVE: Rottnest Island is visited by thousands of private boats each year.

OPPOSITE: Limestone caves are filled with fish and invertebrates.

While many of Australia's best dive sites are remote and difficult to get to, Rottnest Island is virtually in Perth's backyard. Only 18 kilometres north-west of Fremantle (a suburb of Perth), Rottnest Island is 10 kilometres long and 4 kilometres across at its widest point. The name Rottnest is derived from its original Dutch name which meant 'Rat's Nest', so dubbed because of the large, rat-like marsupials called quokkas which are still plentiful on the island today.

Completely government-owned, accommodation on Rottnest Island (known as 'Rotto' to the locals) ranges from tent parks and lodges, through individual self-contained bungalows and units, to a small hotel which used to be the holiday home for the Governor of Western Australia in the late 1800s and early 1900s. Being an easy half-hour ferry ride from the mainland, Rottnest Island is exceptionally popular as a day-trip destination, visited by both locals and overseas visitors. It is even more popular as a holiday destination and the bungalows and units are often booked up twelve months in advance. During peak periods, the government has to hold lotteries to ensure that everyone gets a fair go at the accommodation.

The attraction of Rottnest Island is its natural beauty and carefree lifestyle. No motor vehicles (other than island services) are allowed on the island and transportation is via bicycles which can be hired on the island. Few people from the Western world ever experience the peace and quiet of an environment completely devoid of the sound of motors. The silence is disconcerting at first, but easy to get used to.

Rottnest Island is an A Class Reserve (just shy of a National Park) and all flora, fauna and land forms are protected. The accommodation is concentrated on the north-east coastline, and the rest of the island comprises rolling hills studded with low scrubby trees and bushes. Surrounding the island is a necklace of white-sand bays, gently lapped by the aquamarine blue of the Indian Ocean. Only a quick wade away are shallow reefs, just begging to be explored by snorkellers.

A fully-developed holiday destination, visitors can swim, surf, sunbake, bushwalk, fish, have a round of golf, play tennis and, of course, snorkel and scuba dive.

Fish, clear water, kelp and interesting underwater terrain come immediately to mind when visualising Rottnest diving. Composed of limestone, the surrounding waters are

riddled with ledges, swim-throughs and caves. At some sites, the caves and swim-throughs are so numerous that a diver can swim steadily for the entire dive and never enter the same tunnel or cave twice.

Many of the caverns are of impressive proportions and often these massive formations go undetected. Cruising along a ridge covered in kelp flopping back and forth in the surge, first-time visitors rarely realise that the small, unassuming hole they've just passed over most likely opens onto a huge cavern. Every hole begs investigation.

Inside most caves, divers will find small schools of fish, perhaps a resting ray or even a horn shark. Tucked in a corner or deep under a ledge, one can frequently find two of Rottnest's prettiest fish, the western blue devil and harlequin rock cod. The blue devil is a brilliant blue with iridescent spots and the harlequin rock cod is an equally brilliant red-orange with blue and yellow spots. Both are highly territorial and popular with divers as, when approached, they tend to stand their ground rather than swim away.

Rottnest Island is bathed by a body of water known as the Leeuwin Current which sweeps down from warmer latitudes further north. Rottnest is home to almost 100 species of tropical marine life such as parrotfish, lionfish, foxfish and even the occasional eagle ray, as well as tropical invertebrates such as banded coral shrimp.

The shadowy areas under ledges and along the walls of caves are almost always coated with sponges, ascidians and

corals, plus colourful nudibranchs, some of which are so similar to the surrounding encrusting growth that, at first, you don't even realise you're looking at nudibranchs. It's only on closer inspection that you see there are many, many nudibranchs nestled in amongst the corals and sponges.

Rottnest Island is also home to many species of pelagic fish including cod, jewfish, sweep, trevally and tailor. Frequently, divers are mauled by schools of buffalo bream. Swirling in by the hundreds, these large fish frantically pick through the kelp, often surrounding divers like circling barracuda. Then, as quickly as they arrived, they depart.

Rottnest Island is also home to approximately 12 shipwrecks with the two most popular only minutes from the main jetty. Resting in 3 to 6 metres of water, both the *Denton Holme* and the *Macedon* went down in the late 1800s. There was no loss of life on either ship (except livestock) and both captains were found guilty of negligence. Situated only 20 metres apart, divers can visit both wrecks on the same dive. The sides of the *Macedon* along with the decking frames are still intact. The *Denton Holme* is mostly rubble, although one part of the bow is still intact. Pieces of porcelain, broken bottles and clay smoking pipes can be found amongst the wreckage. All shipwrecks around Rottnest Island are protected by the *Historic Shipwrecks Act*. Divers are welcome to visit the sites but nothing can be removed and care must be taken to avoid damaging the wrecks. Most shipwrecks have underwater plaques nearby describing the ship and the circumstances of its demise.

While there are some deeper reefs, most Rottnest diving is relatively shallow, and one could spend a week at Rotto without exceeding 18 metres. Many of the more beautiful sites are in less than 10 metres. The diving is easy and most of the popular sites are within half-an-hour of the main wharf.

Diving Rottnest takes two forms. Fremantle and Perth dive operators offer double dives via large, fast vessels which make the crossing in less than an hour. These charters are a full day, diving once in the morning, followed by lunch, a surface interval, and a second dive in the afternoon.

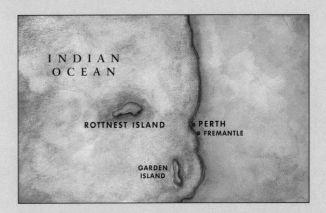

There is only one dive operator on the island itself, who enjoys a booming business. Dive gear can be hired at the shop, or you can take your own. Personal gear can be washed and stored at the shop overnight. Divers with camera gear may wish to hire small trailers for their bicycles, making transfer of camera gear from room to shop a breeze.

While the diving around Rottnest is exciting, visitors should allow a few days for snorkelling, exploring the island and soaking up the carefree lifestyle.

ABOVE: Rottnest Island has many caves and swim-throughs.

OPPOSITE: Zebra fish can be found in large schools.

BOTTOM LEFT: Harlequin rock cod.

BOTTOM RIGHT: Western blue devil fish.

TRAVEL TIPS

GETTING THERE: Fly to Perth and take the ferry.

BEST TIME TO GO: Spring through autumn (October–April). Mid-summer (December–January) has the strongest winds, but these are mostly in the afternoon. Winter (June–August) generally brings big swells and most dive sites are too turbulent to dive. Avoid official holiday periods.

CLIMATE: 18–35°C from summer through autumn (November–April), 15–25°C from winter through spring (May–October).

WATER TEMPERATURES: Summer through autumn, 19–24°C. Winter through spring, 17–20°C.

VISIBILITY: 30+ metres in late summer and autumn; 10–20 metres average.

SNORKELLING: Excellent.

OPERATORS

On the island
MALIBU ROTTNEST DIVE
Tel: (08) 9292 5111, Fax: (08) 9292 5055
Email: malibu@rottnestdiving.com.au
Internet: www.rottnestdiving.com.au

From the mainland
DIVING VENTURES
Tel: (08) 9430 5130, Fax: (08) 9430 5641
Email: diving@dventures.com.au
Internet: www.dventures.com.au

Ferries
BOAT TORQUE 2000
Reservations: 1300 368 686
Perth Terminal: (08) 9221 5844
Fremantle Terminal: (08) 9430 5844

WHALE SHARKS

ABOVE: Ningaloo Reef spans 260 kilometres and is a marine park.

OPPOSITE: Snorkellers swim with a small, slow-moving whale shark.

Whale sharks are the largest cold-blooded animals in the world, and can reach lengths of over 18 metres, although 4–12 metres is more common. Their mouths can be up to 1 metre wide and when a whale shark approaches with mouth agape, one can understand why some people believe that the whale shark is the inspiration for the biblical story of Jonah and the Whale.

Although they are true sharks and have thousands of tiny teeth in over 300 rows, whale sharks neither bite nor chew their food. Instead, they cruise the tropical waters of the world looking for large concentrations of zooplankton which they filter out of the water via massive gills. Pussycats with thyroid problems, whale sharks pose no threat to humans, although being anywhere near a tail when one decides to make a hasty departure wouldn't be a pleasant experience.

Whale sharks are found around the Equator ranging between about 30° North and 35° South. Research on whale sharks is still sketchy but it appears that they prefer surface temperatures between 21–27°C, where cool, nutrient-rich currents mingle with warm, plankton-laden waters. Whale sharks are seen throughout their habitat and they are not considered uncommon, but there's only one place in the world where they are predictable, and that is off Exmouth on the north-west coast of Australia.

Exmouth is a small town of about 3500 people situated 1270 kilometres north of Perth, Western Australia. The area is breathtakingly beautiful, with a hot semi-arid climate and a classic rugged Australian outback terrain. Nearby countryside features wild camels, emus and, of course, kangaroos.

Adjacent to Exmouth is Ningaloo Reef. Stretching 260 kilometres from North-West Cape to just south of Coral Bay at Amherst Point, Ningaloo Reef is the largest fringing reef in the world. It is also one of the most accessible reefs. At its furthest point, it is only 7 kilometres offshore; at its closest, it's only 200 metres from the mainland. A mass coral spawning on Ningaloo Reef every March and April kicks off a chain of biological events, including the arrival of whale sharks. Since the recognition of mass coral spawning on Ningaloo in 1984 and the correlation with large numbers of whale sharks (first recognised in the early 1990s), a whole diving industry has been developed around these marine monsters.

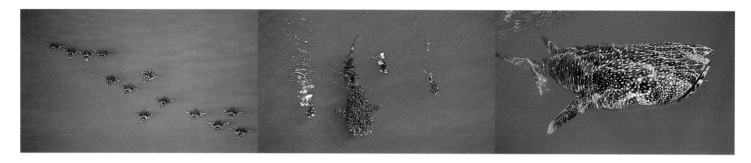

Snorkelling with whale sharks is exciting and tests your fitness. Most charters are land-based and every morning you board your boat to head out to the reef. The only reliable way of finding whale sharks is with the use of a spotter plane. Once a shark is spotted, the pilot radios the boats.

Whale sharks are fully protected under the *Wildlife Conservation Act* and after several years of experience and cooperation between the operators and the government, an excellent set of guidelines has been developed. The spotter plane works for several boats. Once a shark is spotted, the first vessel within a 250-metre radius of the animal is considered to be 'in contact' with the animal and has exclusive rights to the shark for 90 minutes. Other boats can wait their turn if they wish, but only from a significant distance.

The first thing the boat does is plant a 'swimmer' on the shark. The swimmer is a super-fit member of the crew who can swim at a reasonable clip for hours. Having been dropped off in front of the shark, the swimmer moves alongside the animal, marking its position. Because the sharks usually swim several feet under the surface, they are difficult to see from a distance, so having a swimmer to mark the shark is essential in any whale shark operation.

Once the shark is marked, the boat is quickly repositioned about 30 metres in front of the shark. By this point,

snorkellers are standing on the duckboard fully geared with fins, masks and snorkels, ready to jump in. Everyone makes a final check on where the swimmer is, and when the skipper shouts 'Go!', the first group jumps in, taking a bearing on the swimmer, and swimming like crazy in that direction.

Nothing will prepare you for your first encounter with a whale shark. Not only are they long, they're also very wide, especially the head which is all you see at first as it barrels down on you. Most feeding takes place in late afternoon and evening, but sometimes you'll get one with its mouth open during the day, filtering gallons of water as it moves.

Pilot fish and juvenile golden trevally often congregate around the shark's head, and large shark-like cobias and black kingfish sometimes use the whale shark to stalk smaller fish which make up the shark's entourage. Hiding behind and under the whale shark, the cobias and kingfish dart out to attack their prey. Cobias are not dangerous to swimmers, but they look very sharky.

Large ridges along the length of the whale shark's body look just like a steel frame covered with a thin skin. Swimming with a slow, side-to-side motion of its tail, one can't help but think this is some sort of science fiction robo-shark and not an animal which has been around for many thousands of years.

If the whale shark is slow enough, you may be able to keep up for a while, duck diving occasionally to get a better view; but after a minute or two, you'll be exhausted and the shark will slowly pass you. At this point, your boat, which is once again in front of the shark, drops off the next group of snorkellers and then picks up the first group. The boat continues to circle in this way, dropping and retrieving, until the shark sounds or the boat's 90 minutes has expired and it has to move off to allow the next boat to have a go. Hopefully by that time, the plane has located another shark and your boat takes off to find it.

Whale sharks are the highest priority on whale shark charters so few other diving experiences will be had during that time, but often guests are treated to some amazing auxiliary action. Large schools of manta rays are common and snorkellers may even see large balls of tiny baitfish. This can get pretty wild. The whale sharks are swimming through the balls, gulping up the small fish, and sometimes more toothy species of sharks are getting in on the action, too. These situations can be dangerous and you should take advice from the crew on whether it's safe to jump in.

Sometimes you will encounter massive schools of jellyfish. Swimming through them is like swimming through partially-set jelly. And then there was the time a group jumped in on a newly spotted shark only to discover it was a large tiger shark! It's heart-pumping stuff.

OPPOSITE TOP LEFT: Squadron of manta rays.

OPPOSITE TOP CENTRE: Snorkellers with a whale shark.

OPPOSITE TOP RIGHT: A young whale shark.

OPPOSITE BOTTOM LEFT: A whale shark scoops up plankton.

OPPOSITE BOTTOM CENTRE: A whale shark in silhouette.

OPPOSITE BOTTOM RIGHT: Large gills filter water all day.

TRAVEL TIPS

GETTING THERE: Fly to Perth and then connect to Learmonth airport—35 kilometres south of Exmouth.
BEST TIME TO GO: Whale shark season runs from March until June. Best between mid-April to end May.
CLIMATE: Ranges from 20–33°C for the March to June period, with March being the warmest month.
WATER TEMPERATURES: Averages 24–27°C.
VISIBILITY: 20–30 metres, but 5–15 metres is usual.

OPERATORS

VILLAGE DIVE
Tel: (08) 9949 1101, Fax: (08) 9949 1402
Internet: www.exmouthdiving.com or
www.exmouthvillage.com

NORTH STAR CHARTERS
Tel: (08) 9192 1829, Fax: (08) 9192 1830
Email: cruise@NorthStarCharters.com.au
Internet: www.NorthStarCharters.com.au

EXMOUTH DIVING CENTRE
Tel: (08) 9949 1201, Fax: (08) 9949 1680
Email: whaleshark@exmouthdiving.com.au
Internet: www.exmouthdiving.com.au

DIVING VENTURES
Tel: (08) 9430 5130, Fax: (08) 9430 5641
Email: diving@dventures.com.au
Internet: www.dventures.com.au

ROWLEY SHOALS

ABOVE: Adult bannerfish
are almost always
found in pairs.

OPPOSITE: Rowley Shoals
is famous for its colourful
corals and lots of fish.

Rowley Shoals consists of three coral atolls situated 280 kilometres north-west of Broome in northern Western Australia. Formed more than 10 million years ago when the western continental shelf subsided, the three atolls are strikingly similar in dimension, shape, orientation and distance apart. Each is approximately 15 kilometres long and 7–9 kilometres wide; each features a large, deep lagoon surrounded by a fringing coral rim; and each has natural channels cutting through the north-east corner of the reef.

Rowley Shoals is extremely remote and rarely visited. The distance from shore protects it from casual visitors and the summer cyclone season (December to April) prevents access altogether for almost half a year. Part of Rowley Shoals is protected under the direction of the Western Australian Department of Conservation and Land Management and the rest has been declared a marine park. Fishing is limited in most areas and completely banned in others. The number of charter tour operators visiting Rowley's is also strictly controlled. This combination of natural and legislative controls results in less than a few hundred divers visiting the area each year, and the dive sites are virtually untouched.

Most of the dives are wall dives. Starting at the surface, the drop is nearly vertical, plunging down to almost 400 metres in some spots. Huge 4-metre tides (which can get up to 9 metres in the spring) push massive amounts of nutrient rich water along the walls creating a perfect habitat for colourful fans and soft corals which grow surprisingly large in quite shallow water. Most notably, large soft coral trees, which normally exist only in 30+ metres of water, grow happily in only 12 metres at Rowley Shoals.

Cruising the walls are large tuna, marlin, sharks and schooling pelagic fish such as barracuda and trevally. Massive schools of humphead parrotfish and Maori wrasse are also quite common. Closer to the wall are reef fish such as angelfish, coral trout and many, many anemonefish. In all, more than 680 species of marine fish can be found in Rowley Shoals, most of them in profusion.

The dramatic walls are punctuated by sandy bays, probably carved out by the swirling volumes of water which pour over the top of the reef during outgoing tides. Scattered throughout the bays are coral bommies, pinnacles, with maze-like gutters winding through

them. These areas are home to colourful invertebrates such as encrusting corals, sponges, hydroids and bryozoa, plus small crabs, shrimps and nudibranchs, and the ever-present profusion of fish.

Dive trips to Rowley Shoals are always via liveaboard boats and it is strongly recommended that guests rest up before visiting the area because it's non-stop action. Wake up after a restful night on the glassy calm waters inside the lagoon, grab a quick bowl of cereal to keep you going and head out to the dive deck. If you're at Clerke Reef, you might want to have a quiet wake-up snorkel right under the boat where a couple of friendly Maori wrasse and a giant barracuda frequently hang out.

Depending on the day's schedule, early risers might zoom off in the dinghy for an inspiring snorkel on the inner fringing reef. One spot on Clerke Reef, called The Aquarium, is a maze of coral outcrops full of juvenile fish and shells. Usually dead calm and protected from currents, snorkelling there in the first light of morning is a magic experience.

Sometimes the first scuba dive of the day is via dinghies at a site near the mouth of the boat channel. If the tide is going out, drop in near the mouth, and drift through the last section of the channel. Near the end on the ocean side, huge schools of fish hang effortlessly in the current, feeding either on plankton or smaller, unsuspecting fish which are too intent on feeding themselves to notice a predator sneaking up behind them. Once through the channel, head down to check out the huge fans and coral trees.

After the wake-up snorkel or dive, it's time for the boat to leave the lagoon and visit dive sites further afield. Keep a sharp eye out as you travel along the outside perimeter of the reef for humpback whales which migrate through Rowley Shoals during the September through December dive season.

The next couple of dives will probably be walls. In each instance, check out the impressive corals and fans in the deeper water, but make sure to spend a few minutes at your maximum depth simply peering out towards the open ocean. There's a good chance you'll see tuna and sharks, including the occasional oceanic white tip and hammerhead. You may even see a sailfin if you're really lucky. As you work your way up the wall, you'll pass sea whips, more fans, more soft corals and fish in such impressive numbers that they form clouds over the reef.

Closer to the surface, check out the many gutters which cut deeply into the reef. Sometimes large pelagics such as giant trevally can be spotted resting under dark overhangs

or in little caves. Very near the surface, you'll probably be visited by several friendly batfish, which seem to be present on almost every dive.

Dives at Rowley Shoals are almost always one-way dives with the boat dropping off divers at one spot and picking everyone up further along the wall. Often there are slight currents but these are usually insufficiently strong to prevent divers from taking their time and having a good look around. But on occasions, the current can really kick in, and in these conditions, the crew usually organises a full-on, screaming drift dive. Forget your camera, forget your torch and just give in to the sensation of flying across the lush reef. Huge fans quiver to the point of almost snapping off at the base, and whips and soft corals are virtually flattened. It's amazing how long a tank of air lasts when you don't have to kick.

In the late afternoon, your boat will head back to the lagoon where it will anchor for the night. If the tides are right, you'll be treated to one of the most amazing experiences you're ever likely to have—a drift snorkel through the boat channels. When the 4-metre tide starts receding, an amazing volume of water rushes out of the lagoon, funnelling forcefully through the small channels.

Starting on the lagoon side, snorkellers drop in and begin gently drifting down the channel. At first it doesn't seem too strong, but as the channel narrows, your speed picks up and before you know it, you're rocketing. The first time is a bit disconcerting, and you'll be convinced

ABOVE: Rowley Shoals has its own cod hole where large friendly potato cod interact with divers.

OPPOSITE LEFT: Slow-moving dog-faced pufferfish can be found in the oceanside bays.

OPPOSITE RIGHT: Strong currents contribute towards the profusion of healthy corals at shallow depths.

middle of the channel. Other times you might spot small sharks or even a turtle napping in the eddies. On one of the longer straights, take a big breath, duck dive down and kick like crazy. You'll move faster and further underwater than you ever dreamed possible and all in complete silence. It's the closest thing yet to having gills.

After three or four runs through the channel, everyone is pretty tired and it's time to head back to the boat. By sunset, the water inside the lagoon is once again mirror flat and some guests might choose to do a little sunset scurfing, kind of a cross between surfing and skiing using a small surfboard pulled by high-speed dinghies. If you're at Clerke Reef, you might prefer a sunset visit to Bedwell Island. It takes about an hour to stroll the circumference leisurely. Look in the little bird-sized grottos for red-tailed tropic birds, so named for the long red feathers in their tails.

you're either going to be bashed into the rocks, or be dragged uncontrollably across the top of the reef. But neither happens. Invariably, the group splits up and before you know it, it's just you and the fish. Sometimes you'll encounter a school of fish hanging motionlessly in the

Visiting Rowley Shoals is a privilege. Few places in the world can rival either the massive quantities of fish life or the vibrant colours. The brilliant aquamarine of the Indian

Ocean has to be seen to be believed, especially when it is contrasted against the white sand of Bedwell Island. Less than a handful of charter boats visit Rowley Shoals each year and spending a whole week without seeing another vessel is the norm, not the exception. Rowley Shoals is very special, indeed!

ABOVE: Snorkelling the boat channel is great fun.

OPPOSITE TOP: Large manta rays can be seen in the open sea.

OPPOSITE BOTTOM: Sharks can be seen on virtually every dive.

BELOW: Happy divers waiting to jump in for another drift dive.

TRAVEL TIPS

GETTING THERE: Rowley Shoals can only be visited via liveaboard vessels. Most operate out of Broome, Western Australia.

BEST TIME TO GO: Due to monsoons, the dive season is limited to spring and early summer (September–early December).

CLIMATE: 24–31°C at Rowley Shoals, much warmer in Broome.

WATER TEMPERATURES: 25–29°C with some colder thermoclimes down deep.

VISIBILITY: Regularly 40 to 60+ metres on incoming tides. Visibility drops significantly on outgoing tides.

SNORKELLING: Excellent snorkelling with good opportunities on practically every dive.

OPERATORS

NORTH STAR CHARTERS
Tel: (08) 9192 1829, Fax: (08) 9192 1830
Email: cruise@NorthStarCharters.com.au
Internet: www.NorthStarCharters.com.au

PEARL SEA COASTAL CRUISES
Tel: (08) 9192 3829, Fax: (08) 9193 5785
Email: enquiry@pearlseacruises.com
Internet: www.pearlseacruises.com

OCEANIC CHARTERS
Tel: (08) 9193 6679, Fax: (08) 9193 6679
Email: oceanic@oceaniccruises.com.au
Internet: www.oceaniccruises.com.au

PRACTICALITIES

TIPPING: In Australia, tipping is neither required nor expected. In taxis, passengers will often round up to the nearest dollar for ease of payment. When dining out, they might put a dollar or two on the table after a meal. Tipping on liveaboard boats is also unnecessary. If you liked the crew, buy them a drink when you get back to shore.

CLIMATE: Average temperatures are given in each chapter, but for more detailed and up-to-the-minute information on climate throughout Australia, visit www.bom.gov.au/climate.

TELEPHONE NUMBERS: Telephone numbers in Australia are generally eight digits with a two-digit area code beginning with zero, for example, (02) 9665 6890. All cellular phone numbers begin with a four-digit network prefix beginning with zero and then a six-digit number (for example 0419 625 797). When calling from overseas, dial '61' for the country code, then all the numbers except the leading zero (for example 61 2 9665 6890). The *White Pages* and *Yellow Pages* directories can be found on the Internet at www.telstra.com.

SCHOOL TERMS AND HOLIDAYS: Australian children attend four terms per school year (three terms in Tasmania) with a short break between each term. The summer break is the end of the school year and lasts around two months from December through January. Australia's peak travel periods are during school holidays and many destinations are booked out. Overseas travellers should avoid travelling during school holidays. Details of the school terms in all the states can be found at: www.australiatrade.com.au/Events

WETSUIT CONVERSIONS

3mm	⅛ inch (3mm is slightly thinner)
5mm	3/16 inch (5mm is slightly thicker)
7mm	¼ inch (7mm is slightly thicker)

TEMPERATURE

DEPTH

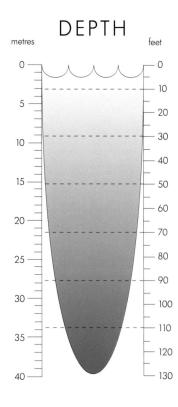

CONTRIBUTING AUTHORS

ALAN BECKHURST (Wilsons Promontory)

Born in Melbourne, Alan has had a lifelong fascination with the sea. After years of freediving, spearfishing and hundreds of scuba dives around Australia, he still dives most weekends locally with his wife, Mary. Both are passionate about diving in Victoria and have their own boat at Queenscliff. His two children are grown, and Alan is looking forward to spending even more time underwater filming and photographing.

Alan expresses his fervour for being on or under the sea by writing for books, magazines and newsletters. He is a keen 'Club' man, and a delegate to the Scuba Divers Federation of Victoria, a position which allows him to actively participate in the protection of divers' rights.

MARY MALLOY (Port Phillip Heads)

Since learning to dive in 1983 in Victoria, Mary has logged over 1000 dives. As well as other parts of Australia, Mary has dived the Great Barrier Reef, Papua New Guinea, Fiji, and the Solomon Islands, yet her favourite dive area is still Port Phillip Heads, near Melbourne, in Victoria.

In 1985, Mary took up underwater photography, which has now grown beyond a hobby, and her images have appeared in many publications. Her career highlight would have to be photographing a white shark without a cage, and then having the image published in *National Geographic* magazine. Her business, Nitrographics, continues to sell images via repeat business and through her website, www.nitrographics.com.au

MARK SPENCER (Eaglehawk)

Mark Spencer learned to dive in 1974 and is best-known for his adventure diving and self-imposed challenging projects. Two such projects were the photo-documentation of the SS *Catterthun*, a deep water wreck off Seal Rocks, in New South Wales, and McCavity's Cave, a remote, almost inaccessible flooded limestone cave in Wellington, New South Wales. Both projects featured in *Australian Geographic* magazine.

In 1997–98, Mark led expeditions to Turkey to verify the identity and to photo-document the AE2 submarine, an Australian submarine which was scuttled during the Gallipoli campaign in World War I, and now rests in 72 metres of water.

After nearly 26 years of total immersion, Mark's current project is a series of panorama posters exploring the relationship between Australians and the sea. These photos are taken at the land/sea interface, and his best-known image in this series is entitled 'Bondi Beach', which can be viewed at his website: www.australia-downunder-productions.com.

NEIL VINCENT (Mount Gambier)

Neil Vincent is a highly qualified and experienced cave diver who has extensively explored caves in the Nullarbor Plain, Mount Gambier and New South Wales. Equally important to him are shallower, non-technical dives where he can relax and spend long hours exploring the mysteries of the sea and the fascinating behaviour of marine life.

Neil is a talented underwater photographer and has won many photography competitions in Australia and overseas. He is also an accomplished writer and is a regular contributor to airline, adventure travel and dive magazines around the world.

Neil believes in the 'work hard, play hard' ethic and there are few weekends when you won't see him, along with his equally accomplished wife, Lyn, under the water getting truly wet.

ABOUT THE PHOTOGRAPHY

Underwater photography is not easy, but I have discovered over the years that it can be a whole lot easier if you invest in good equipment. I use Nikon cameras exclusively and I am constantly amazed by their robustness and reliability. My battery of lenses includes the 60 mm, 105 mm, 2x teleconverter (which gives me the equivalent of a 200 mm lens), 35–70 zoom, 24 mm, 20 mm, 14 mm and 16 mm fish-eye, and I have used every single one of them to produce this book.

I house my cameras in aluminium Subal housings made in Austria. The original compact housing and still the best. Subal housings feature a sturdy design, high-quality finish, access to almost all the controls on my cameras and, most importantly, exceptionally fine after-sales service and support in the form of Sea Optics in South Australia.

I own four Ikelite Substrobe 200s. Without question, these are the finest strobes available to underwater photographers. Their exceptional power, immediate recycle time, TTL function, small size, light weight and ni-cad power packs which recharge in less than an hour using Ikelite's fabulous Smart Charger, make the Substrobe 200 ideal for the heavy demands I place on my equipment.

My armoury includes Technical Lighting Control (TLC) strobe arms, invented by American nature photographer, Tom Campbell and now owned and distributed by Nikon. With the placement of strobes so critical in underwater photography, I believe that the articulated TLC design is the single most important invention for underwater photography since the introduction of the Nikonos 15 mm lens. Finally, we can position our strobes where they should be, and not where it's easiest. I can say, without hesitation, that my photography has improved by orders of magnitude since I bought my TLC strobe arms.

I use Fuji's Velvia film (rated at ISO 40) exclusively for close-up and rated at ISO 100 for topside work. Nothing comes close to the supersaturation and extreme crispness of the film. For wide-angle underwater, I use Kodak's Ektachrome 100 VS. Once again, I am attracted to the saturated colours, but also to the way it handles blue, in my opinion producing a bright colour slightly warmer than the Fuji films. Ektachrome 100 VS also pushes beautifully and is my favourite ISO 200 film.

Camera equipment is important, but when it comes to underwater photography, the dive gear is equally important. When I'm concentrating on my photography, the last thing I want to think about is my diving equipment, and depending on the difficulty of the shoot, sometimes the last thing I'm able to think about is my dive gear. So I use only the very best which is Japan's Apollo Prestige. The entire line is high performance, super comfortable and exceptionally durable. Not only do I use Apollo exclusively, but I kit out my models in Apollo as well, and they always look stunning.

The one exception to Apollo equipment is my polarfibrelined lycra Shark Suit made by the family-owned Australian company, Extreme Australia. In warm water, these are fabulous. They are easy to put on and take off (an energy-saving consideration when you are doing five dives a day!), and feel dry to the touch within minutes, meaning that it feels like I'm putting on a dry suit every time I gear up. When wet, they are slightly negatively buoyant which means I have to wear less weights and my lean, mean models generally wear no weights at all, which also looks great in pictures.

I always travel with two complete systems and generally configure one for close-up and one for wide-angle. This way, I have a better chance of making the most of any single dive. (Topside photographers take note: underwater photographers cannot change lenses or film while underwater.) I have also noticed that I have far fewer floods and equipment problems than my colleagues and, while some of this can be attributed to the quality of my equipment, I also believe that reducing the number of times you reconfigure your equipment, reduces the potential for accidents.

My final secret is to dive lots and shoot lots. I never dive without at least one camera and I rarely pass up an opportunity to dive. You have to be in it to get it. It's that simple!

PHOTOGRAPHY CREDITS

My goal with this book was to represent the selected dive sites as accurately and as completely as space permitted, and in order to achieve this, on occasion, I have had to use photographs taken by other people. I was overwhelmed by the reception I received when I approached my colleagues regarding this project and I am very grateful for their encouragement and generous support.

Barry Andrewartha/Mountain Ocean Travel Publications 123t; Bill and Peter Boyle 83tr, 89, 91r; David Bryant/Sea Pics 83tl; Glen Cowans/Underview-Aquatic & Wildlife Imagery 124, 126; Mike Cufer/Fisheye 9, 93, 94b, 121; Max Gleeson 49, 50, 71b; Karen Gowlett-Holmes 92, 96l, 97, 116; Stefan Harasymow 127; Ken Hoppen/Ken Hoppen Photography 88b, 88t, 91l; Stuart Hutchison 34l, 119; Maria Kavallaris/Sea Dance Images 63; Greg Lee Steere Back Cover, Mary Malloy/Nitrographics 80, 81, 82, 83tc, 84, 86, 87, 88c, 90l, 90r; Jeff Mullins/Reef Images 5, 94t, 134; Peter and Margy Nicholas/Blue Water Images 16, 64c, 125; Mark Norman 15; John Olsen 27, 30r; Becca Saunders/Twilight Zone Photographics Front Cover, 6, 11, 12l, 13, 14, 18l, 18c, 18r, 20, 21, 22t, 22b, 24, 31, 35, 36, 37, 38tr, 38tl, 38b, 38tc, 39t, 39b, 40, 42, 45, 46l, 46c, 51, 52c, 52b, 55, 57, 58t, 58b, 59, 64l, 68r, 68l, 69b, 69c, 70, 72, 74l, 74r, 76bl, 76t, 76br, 77, 78, 96r, 105, 113, 114c, 114r, 114l, 118, 123b, 128, 130c, 137t, 137bl, 137br, 142, 143, 144l, 144r, 145, 146b, 146b, 146t, 147t, 149, 152, 154; Becca Saunders/Auscape International 32, 33, 122; Mark Spencer/Twilight Zone Photographics 2, 10, 12r, 17, 22c, 26, 28, 29, 30l, 41, 44, 46r, 48, 52t, 54, 56b, 56t, 60, 65, 66, 69t, 71t, 73, 75, 76bc, 100, 101, 102b, 102t, 103, 104, 115, 129, 130r, 130l, 132, 135, 136, 138, 139, 140tl, 140tc, 140tr, 140bl, 140bc, 140br, 151, 160, photo of author; Mark Spencer/Auscape International 120; Neil Vincent 34r, 62, 64r, 98, 108l, 109; Robbert Westerdyk 53, 108c; Alex Wyschnja 106, 107, 108r, 110, 112, l=left, r=right, t=top, b=bottom and c=centre

ACKNOWLEDGEMENTS

This book would not have been possible without the help and encouragement of many people. Firstly, thanks to Richard and Jody Taylor for encouraging New Holland Publishers to approach me to write this book. Thanks to Anouska Good for always using fifty words rather than ten and for making me feel so warm and fuzzy. Thanks also to Monica Ban, for her patience while battling both impossible schedules and authors with strong ideas. Thanks also, Monica, for giving in and letting me use the verb 'to sound'.

Although I officially had one year to research and write this book, it is actually the culmination of many years of travel. Thanks to all the operators, hotels and hire car companies who extended their hospitality over the years. There are too many to mention by name, but you know who you are. I hope I've done you proud. Also, a special thanks to Jennifer Randell of the Western Australia Tourism Commission for her overwhelming support. The Western Australia chapters wouldn't be nearly as complete without her extensive help. Thanks also to Dawn and Jeff Mullins for their generous support and continuing friendship. Those days at Busselton and Rottnest were so much fun, even if the weather wasn't that great!

The contributing photographers are acknowledged on page 151, but I would like to thank the many other photographers who actively supported me throughout the project, namely Patrick Baker, Andrew Bowie, David Haines, Graeme Henderson, Jenny Ough, Geoff Paynter, Roberto Rinaldi, Tim Rock, Ian Shaw, Ann Storrie, Alan Wiggs and Mal Yeo. Their photos were excellent and only the limitation of space prevented me from using them all. An extra special thanks to Steve Purvis for his generous support in supplying drawings of shipwrecks. Although I was unable to use them in the book, they helped me enormously as reference materials.

On a more personal note, a great big thank you to my two best friends, Maria and Sophie for their continuing support, to my parents for their unconditional love and most of all, to Mark…for everything.

FURTHER READING

The following are identification books and dive guides which may be of use to readers.

IDENTIFICATION BOOKS

GUIDE TO SEA FISHES OF AUSTRALIA by Rudie Kuiter
Excellent comprehensive reference book covering 950 species. All colour photography, mostly showing fish in their natural habitat. Brief but informative text, plus a distribution map for each species. Softcover, small format, 430 pages.
ISBN 1 86436 091 7

NUDIBRANCHS AND SEA SNAILS INDO-PACIFIC FIELD GUIDE by Helmut Debelius
A definitive guide to nudibranchs including Australia's Great Barrier Reef, Papua New Guinea and the islands of the South Pacific. Quality hardcover, small format, 321 pages.

FISHES OF THE GREAT BARRIER REEF AND CORAL SEA by John E. Randall, Gerald R. Allen and Roger C. Steene
Over 1200 species and 1400 photographs. Superbly written in laymen's terms. Hardcover, large format, 560 pages.
ISBN 1 86333 012 7

MARINE FISHES OF THE GREAT BARRIER REEF AND SOUTH-EAST ASIA by Gerry Allen
An excellent field guide featuring a brief description of each species plus a full colour drawing. Softcover, small format, 298 pages.
ISBN 0 73098 363 3

ANEMONEFISH AND THEIR HOST SEA ANEMONES (FIELD GUIDE TO) by Daphne G. Fautin and Gerald R. Allen
Every species of anemonefish and every species of host anemone is covered in full colour photographs, plus informative text. Softcover, medium format, 160 pages.
ISBN 0 73095 216 9

AUSTRALIAN MARINE LIFE—THE PLANTS AND ANIMALS OF TEMPERATE WATERS by Dr. Graham J. Edgar
A true encyclopedia of Australian temperate marine animals and plants presented in a clear layout with over 1300 colour photographs covering lichens to whales and everything in between. The most concise volume on temperate Australian invertebrates available. Softcover, large format, 544 pages.
ISBN 1 8733 438 X

TROPICAL PACIFIC INVERTEBRATES by Patrick L. Colin and Charles Arneson
An excellent book on tropical invertebrates. The best of several in a similar format. Softcover, medium format, 295 pages.
ISBN 0 96456 250 2

SEA SLUGS OF WESTERN AUSTRALIA by Fred Wells and Clayton Bryce
Nudibranchs plus sea slugs, seahares, pteropods and other marine creatures of the Class Gastropoda, many of which also occur in the eastern states. Full colour. Softcover, small format, 184 pages.
ISBN 0 73095 523 0

SHARKS AND RAYS OF AUSTRALIA by P.R. Last and J.D. Stevens
In-depth descriptions of all sharks and rays found in Australian waters. Each species has a description, drawings, identification keys and worldwide distribution maps. The appendix has 84 colour plates. Hardcover, large format, 600 pages.
ISBN 0 64305 143 0

DIVE GUIDES

DIVING AUSTRALIA—A GUIDE TO THE BEST DIVING DOWN UNDER by Neville Coleman and Nigel Marsh
Excellent overview of diving all over Australia. Thousands of dive sites covered. Brief descriptions with lots of photographs and maps. Softcover, small format, 353 pages.
ISBN 9 62593 104 X

THE DIVE SITES OF THE GREAT BARRIER REEF AND THE CORAL SEA by Neville Coleman
Descriptions of all the popular dive sites on the Great Barrier Reef and the Coral Sea. This book covers the Capricorn and Bunker Groups (Heron Island) up to the far north reefs of Holmes, Bougainville and Osprey. Includes maps. Softcover, small format, 176 pages.
ISBN 1 86436 095 X

FURTHER READING

TOM BYRON'S DIVE GUIDES

A series of books on various areas along the east coast of Australia. Exceptionally detailed, often including landmarks and GPS locations. All are softcover, standard to medium format, and varying pages.
Tom Byron Publications,
Tel: (02) 9774 5965.
Email: tombyron@telstra.easymail.com.au
Internet: www.netspace.net.au/~tombyron

DIVE WESTERN AUSTRALIA by Jeff Mullins

Descriptions of popular dive sites throughout Western Australia. Includes maps, mono photographs and colour plates. Softcover, small format, 65 pages.
ISBN 0 64609 645 1

SHIPWRECKS

Books by Max Gleeson
Max can be contacted at: maxglee@aussiemail.com.au

SS *YONGALA*—TOWNSVILLE'S TITANIC

Everything you would ever want to know about the SS *Yongala* including history, loss and subsequent discovery. Mono and colour photographs. Hardcover, small format, 120 pages.
ISBN 0 64637 781 7

SHIPWRECKS, STORMS AND SEAMEN

Covers 11 shipwrecks along the New South Wales coast, including the *Catterthun* and *Satara*, both mentioned in this book. Meticulously researched, it includes mono and colour photographs and in situ drawings. Softcover, medium format, 168 pages.
ISBN 0 64628 019 8

THE VANISHED FLEET OF THE SYDNEY COASTLINE

Covers 15 shipwrecks along the New South Wales coastline. Thoroughly researched, includes mono and colour photographs and in situ drawings. Softcover, medium format, 168 pages.
ISBN 0 64613 671 2

INDEX

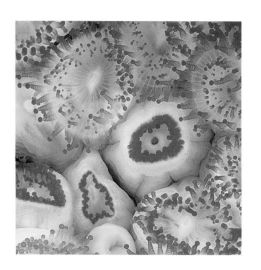